W. Elliot Woodward

Woodward's One Hundred and Eighth Sale

W. Elliot Woodward

Woodward's One Hundred and Eighth Sale

ISBN/EAN: 9783743341920

Manufactured in Europe, USA, Canada, Australia, Japa

Cover: Foto ©ninafisch / pixelio.de

Manufactured and distributed by brebook publishing software
(www.brebook.com)

W. Elliot Woodward

Woodward's One Hundred and Eighth Sale

W. Elliot Woodward's

ONE HUNDRED AND EIGHTH SALE.

Coins & Medals,

AMERICAN AND FOREIGN.

Forbes & Day Collections.

WEDNESDAY, THURSDAY & FRIDAY,

APRIL 16, 17, 18, 1890.

CATALOGUE

OF THE

EXTENSIVE AND IMPORTANT COLLECTIONS

OF

AMERICAN COINS AND MEDALS,

OF

A. FORBES and JOHN H. DAY,

Of ST. LOUIS, MO.

COMPRISING

Colonial Coins, Early Proof Sets, Dollars, Half Dollars, Dimes, Fine Cents and Half Cents, Rare Store Cards, Presidential and other Medals, Foreign Coins and Medals, Numismatic Literature, Cabinets, Etc.

All to be Sold by Auction,

By Messrs. BANGS & CO.,

739 and 741 Broadway, New York City,

WEDNESDAY, THURSDAY AND FRIDAY,

APRIL 16, 17 and 18, 1890.

Coins will be on exhibition at the Auction Rooms, on the days of sale, from 10 A. M. to 1 P. M., and the sale will take place each day promptly at 2 o'clock. Orders for the sale will be carefully and faithfully executed by the Auctioneers and all Coin Dealers.

Catalogue by W. Elliot Woodward.

Assisted by ED. FROSSARD, Esq., of New York City.

BOSTON:

T. R. MARVIN & SON, NUMISMATIC PRINTERS.

1890.

INDEX.

Correspondents are requested to send early orders, thus giving me time to enter them in my books before I leave for New York. It is not an uncommon thing for me to have a greater number of orders than there are lots in the catalogue and many often arrive too late. Writing as I do, with difficulty, it is very desirable that those who wish to entrust their orders to me, should send them as early as possible, that they may receive proper attention. Address as below; but late orders may be sent to me at New York, care of the auctioneers.

The coin dealers of New York, Baltimore, Philadelphia, and Lancaster, Pa., will also receive and faithfully execute bids that may be placed with them. As many inquiries are sent me asking for catalogues to complete files, I have prepared a printed list of those that can be supplied, neatly priced in ink, to the 108th inclusive, which will be sold at prices named. This list will be sent on application.

Priced Catalogues of this sale, printed on heavy tinted paper, will be mailed to order as soon after the sale as possible on receipt of $1.00.

W. ELLIOT WOODWARD,

38 Harlow Street, Dorchester Mass.

CATALOGUE.

FOREIGN MEDALS, ETC.

1 APHRODITE. Medallion bust (30) in ebony frame. 5 x 5½ in.

2 St. Jacob. Berlin iron placque. 3 x 4½ in.

3 Female depositing wreath upon executioner's block. Berlin iron. 3½ in.

4 Medallion bust of Franklin, with ring. Berlin iron. 3¼ in.

5 Classical figures; military bust. Berlin iron. 3 in. 3 pcs.

6 Joseph Chr. Trombelli, Church dignitary, 1776. Bust; rev., naked figure amid flowers. Bronze, cast. Italy. 3 in.

7 A. F. Corius, divine and Prof. of History, 1751. Bust; rev., science rewarded. Bronze cast. 3½ in.

8 Cornelius Van Tromp, Dutch Admiral, 1666. Bust in high relief; rev., Dutch and English ships in action. Bronze cast, ~~fine original~~. 3 in.

9 Japanese Sword Guard, gold decoration; fine. 2 pcs.

10 Japanese Knife Handle, gold and silver decoration; fine. 3¾ in.

11 Leopold I and II, Charles III and VI, etc. Historical medals commemorating victories, treaties of peace, etc., each with bust of Austrian emperor, and all different. Fine lot, all original, one size 20, others 28 to 36. 24 pcs.

2 German States. Russia, Sweden, France. Historical medals, chiefly of last century. Different, w.m., fine. 20 to 32. 30 pcs.

3 Bust of Luther; rev., Faith at altar. 2d Jubilee. W.m., fine. 30.

4 Prussia. Victories over the French, 1813, 1870. W.m., different, fine. 27 to 34. 3 pcs.

5 Thames Tunnel, Karlsbad Springs, etc. W.m., good to fine, one pierced. 16 to 26. 10 pcs.

6 Bust of Pius IX; rev., NE 1792 DECEDE 1878. W.m., with original black ribbon, struck for Canada. 19. 40 pcs.

7 AUSTRIA. Leopold I. Bust r.; rev., views of cities and fortresses captured from the Turks. Bronze, fine. different. 24 and 27. 2 pcs.

8 BAVARIA. Maximilian Joseph. Bust; rev., monument. Bronze, fine. 30.

9 ALBERT DURER. Portrait bust; rev., angel holding tablet with inscription. Bronze cast, issued at Nuremberg in 1828. 33.

0 ENGLAND. Charles, Prince of Wales. Bust r., 1745; rev., figure of Britannia at sea-shore. Bronze, fine, *rare*.

1 George IV. 1821. Coronation medal. Bronze, fine, a little nicked on edge. 22.

2 Victoria. 1851. Bust; rev. commemorates visit to Liverpool and Manchester. Tin, fine. 48.

3 Bust of James, Earl of Charlemont: rev., Britannia seated, holding the Irish shield. Irish Royal Academy medal, 1786. Bronze, fine.

4 William Pitt. Bust; rev., usual inscr. Yellow bronze, damaged by fire. 25.

5 Bust right; rev., FRANCIS HENRY EGERTON EARL OF BRIDGEWATER. Bronze, v. good. 26.

6 FRANCE. Philippe Quinault. Bust; rev., Apollo at sunrise, 1718. Bronze, cast, fine, pierced. 38.

7 Confederation des François. Paris, 1790. Bronze, pierced, good and *rare*. 22.

8 Cardinal Talleyrand. Bust; rev., mortuary inscription, 1821. Bronze, very good. 32.

9 David Leroy, Architect and Member of the French Institute. Bust: rev., column. Year 11. Bronze, good. 26.

Arnold, Boileau, Du Pin, Patrick Hamilton, etc., theologians and academicians. Bronze medalets, each with bust, fine. 18 and 19. 6 pcs.

Napoleon I, Carolina. Bronze medalets, last with Greek inscription. Fine. 16 and 14. 3 pcs.

GENEVA. 3d Jubilee of Reformation, 1833. Bronze, fine. 22. 2 pcs.

GERMANY. Bronze medal, emblematic of marital felicity. Very fine. 24.

Von Rudloff, Director of Postal service. Bust; rev., inscription commemorative of his 50 years' service in the P. O. Dept., 1850. Bronze, good. 27.

HAVANA. Medal of the Royal Cigar Manufactory of La Honradez. Bronze gilt, fine. 36.

ITALY. Ferdinand III, Grand Duke of Tuscany. Mortuary medal with bust, 1824. Bronze, very good. 32.

Vincentius Gravina. Fine bronze medal, with bust, Rome, 1805. 42.

Joannes Galeatius. Bust; rev., view of the cathedral at Milan. Bronze gilt, mint state. 30.

Papal States. Julius I and III, Benedict XIV, Pius IX. Bronze medals, four with busts. Fine. 22 to 24. 5 pcs.

Vincentius Riccatus, Hercules Gonzalvi, etc. Cardinals and Church dignitaries. Bronze, fine. 25 to 33. 5 pcs.

Venice. View of the Railroad Bridge erected in 1841. Bronze, fine. 33.

MEXICO. Bust r.: rev., female seated. Bronze medal of the Mexican Academy. Good. 32.

Mexican Church medals, one with figure of St. Philip, the other with that of Our Lady of Guadalupe, 1805. Oval, silvered bronze and brass, fair and good. 21 and 20. 3 pcs.

NETHERLANDS. Figure of Aesculapius; rev., altar, surmounted by crowned shield. Medal of the Botanical Gardens of the Academy of Medicine, 1729. Brass cast, fine and scarce. 31.

POLAND. Bust of Stanislaus I; rev., monument. Bronze, very good. 32.

SAXE-COBURG. Marriage medal of Ernest, hereditary prince, and of Alexandrina, princess of Baden, 1842. Busts jugata; rev., quadriga. Bronze, fine. 26.

47 SPAIN. Busts of Charles III and of members of the royal family; rev., mining scene. Bronze medal, issued by the Metal Mining Society of Spain. Bronze, good, pierced, *rare*. 40.

48 SWEDEN. Charles IX. Bust r.; rev., four chained pillars crowned, 1682. Fine silver medal with gilt ring. 32.

49 Christina. Bust to knees, holding orb, sceptre and crown; rev., blank. Trial impression of a rare crown: copper, fine. 30.

50 Gustavus III. Bust r.: rev., inscription in 13 lines, 1772. Very fine. 40.

51 STRASBOURG. Bust of Erwin von Steinbach; rev., view of the cathedral. Bronze, good. 29.

52 Bronze medals. Austria, Germany, France, etc., several of historical interest. Fine. 17 to 30. 16 pcs.

53 Brass medals. Frederic the Great, Francis of Austria, and Alexander of Russia, etc. Good to fine, one pierced. 19 to 31. 10 pcs.

54 FOREIGN MEDALS. Bronzed, casts, electros, etc. Lot includes several obsidional coins, copies of rare medals, etc., several very large. 70 pcs.

55 MASONIC MEDALS. Radiant sun over square, compasses and gavel, DOCH DER SEGEN KOMMT VON OBEN 26 JUNI 1853; rev., inscription to commemorate the festival of Mayer's twenty-fifth year's service as Master of Lodge at Hamm. Copper, pierced, very fairly preserved and of great rarity. 28. Marvin 510.

56 Masonic Ducat, struck in silver. Very fine. M. 12.

57 St. Alexander, Paris. Radiant triangle; rev., sun rising over mountain. Masonic emblems in foreground. Bronze, very fine. M. 135.

58 Parfait Accord, Ville Franche, Rhone. Two right hands joined; rev., level. Brass. 18. Very good for this piece, which is scarce. M. 345.

59 Brass planchet, engraved in relief; square, compasses and gavel, "Paix.·. Union.·. Regeneration.·. (1833)"; rev., similarly cut, "Societe d'Agriculture," etc. Size 20. Evidently designed for a stamp or book-die; curious.

60 Amis Reunis. Officer's jewel, triangle enclosing clasped hands and name of Lodge engraved; with original ribbon. From Crepy collection.

61 L'Aurore Naissante, Frankfort. Bijou, or member's badge; a cluster of formal rays with ring; on centre a triangle with name of Lodge and upper half of sun's face resting on lower bar; rev. incused. Gilt. Size 26.

These two "jewels" differ greatly in style from those worn by American Lodges, and are interesting as showing Continental Masonic customs. Very few are to be found in America, and all, we believe, came from the Crepy collection.

63 COPPER COINS. Austria, Barbadoes, England (half far. 1844), France, German States, Ionian Islands, Mexico, Oriental, etc. Desirable for selections; very fair to fine. 60 pcs.

64 Another lot. Poor, many pierced. 48 pcs.

65 English Tradesmen's Halfpenny Tokens. Very good and fine. 5 pcs.

66 Dominica, 1877; Mitad, 1874; Belin, ¼ Real; Ferrocahil de la Bahia. Copper, brass, and w.m., uncir. 8 pcs.

67 Spain. Charles IV. Paper Dollars. 2 pcs.

68 Sweden. Charles XII. Copper Dalers, nine varieties. Poor to fine. 10 pcs.

69 Jetons, Tokens, Weights, etc. Copper and brass, poor to fine, several pierced. 59 pcs.

70 Communion Tokens. St. Paul's Church, Montreal (star-shaped); St. Andrew's Church, Quebec; Communion Table; rev., "This do in remembrance of Me" (6). Very good and fine, scarce. 8 pcs.

71 Collection of Japanese Bronze Coins, from earliest period to the present time. All in separate boxes, with name of rulers, etc. Average as fine as found. 133 pcs.

AMERICAN COINS.

72 1794 Dollar. Fine for date, the stars to l. and "United States" on rev. weak as usual; has been pierced and skillfully plugged between B E of "Liberty." Desirable specimen; *rare.*

73 1796 Dollar. Very fine, nicked over the ear, scarce.

74 1853 Dollar. Fine.

75 1873 Trade Dollar, *San Francisco m.* ~~Fine.~~

76 1878 Pattern Dollar. Morgan's design. Brilliant proof.

77 1879 Pattern Dollar. Same obverse as last; rev., eagle with drooping wings holds a branch of laurel and three arrows, UNITED STATES OF AMERICA ONE DOLLAR, IN GOD WE TRUST, in curving lines. Brilliant proof; very *rare.*

78 1879 Pattern Dollar. Small head of Liberty to left, IN GOD WE TRUST above, seven stars to l. and six to r.; rev., small eagle in half wreath, E PLURIBUS UNUM in very small letters above. Proof impression, slightly hay-marked. *Very rare.*

79 1879 Metric Pattern Dollar. Bust with beaded coronet; rev., composition and weight within beaded circle, above which DEO EST GLORIA in small characters. *Copper* proof; *rare.*

80 1879 Goloid Metric Dollar. Usual obv.; rev., composition and weight in circle of stars, around which GOLOID METRIC DOLLAR, DEO EST GLORIA. Mint state; *rare.*

81 1880 Goloid Metric Dollar. Same type as last, but *copper* proof. *Very rare.*

82 1806 Half Dollar. Pointed 6 in date; very good.

83 1807 Half Dollar. Head to right. Very fair; pierced.

84 1807 Half Dollar. Head to left; ~~very good~~.

85 1809 Half Dollar. Good.

86 1817 over '13. Half Dollar. Fair; scarce.

87 1821 Quarter Dollar. Very good.

88 1883 Quarter Dollar. Brilliant proof.

89 1796 Dime. Poor, date visible, scarce.

90 Dimes. 1805, 1814, 1820, 1821, 1823, 1824, 1825, 1827, 1828, 1834, 1837, 1844, 1853. Poor to v. good. 18 pcs.

91 1883 Dime. Fine proof.

92 1829–1844. Half Dimes. Consecutive and varieties. Poor to fine. 23 pcs.

93 1873 Half Dime, ~~without arrows~~. Proof.

94 Three Cents. 1851, 1854. Very good. 2 pcs.

95 1879 Minor Proof Set. 1, 3, 5 Cents. Brilliant proofs. 2 sets.

96 1881 Same. 1, 3, 5 Cents. Brilliant proofs. 3 sets.

97 1881 Duplicates. 3 sets.

98 1881 Duplicates. 3 sets.

99 1881 Duplicates. 4 sets.

100 1883 1, 3, 5 (3 varieties) Cents. Brilliant proofs. 5 pcs.

101 1883 Duplicates. 2 sets.

102 1883 Duplicates. 2 sets.

103 1883 1, 3, and 5 (2 varieties) Cents. Fine proofs. 4 pcs.

104 1884 1, 3, 5 Cents. Brilliant proofs. 2 sets.

105 1884 Duplicates. 2 sets.

106 1884 Duplicates. 2 sets.

107 Five Cents Nickel. 1866, 1867 (var.), 1868–1876, 1882. Very fine. 13 pcs.

108 Two Cents Bronze. 1864, 1865, 1866, 1868, 1871, 1872. Good to fine. 7 pcs.

109 1793 Wreath Cent. Lettered edge; poor.

110 1802 Cent; rev., stemless wreath. Very fair.

111 1803 Cent. Good.

112 1804 Genuine Cents, but altered dates. Poor and fair. 4 pcs.

113 1807 over '06. Cent. Good, nicked on cheek.

114 1810 over '09. Cent. Good, but dark green.

115 1817 Cent. Fine.

116 1818 Cent. Connected stars; uncirculated.

117 1818 Cents. Duplicates. Fine. 2 pcs.

118 1820 Cent. Connected stars. Bright red; uncirculated.

119 1820 Cents. Same condition. 2 pcs.

120 1820 Cents. Nearly bright red; uncirculated. 4 pcs.

121 1820 Cents. Not quite as fine as last. 5 pcs.

122 1844, 1845, 1846. Cents. Very good and fine. 3 pcs.

123 1850 Cents. Bright red; uncirculated. 4 pcs.

124 1850 Cents. Bright red; uncirculated. 4 pcs.

125 1850 Cents. Reddish; fine and uncirculated. 5 pcs.

126 1852 Cents. Bright red; uncirculated. 3 pcs.

127 1852 Cents. Nearly same condition. 3 pcs.

128 1858 Cents. Very fine. 7 pcs.

129 1796–1856 Cents. Lot includes 1823. Poor to very good, 5 pierced. 25 pcs.

130 1793 Half Cent. Very good: slightly corroded.

131 Half Cents. 1794 (?), 1797, 1804, 1806, 1807, 1809, 1826, 1828. Poor to very good, one pierced. 14 pcs.

132 1835 Half Cents. Very fine. 12 pcs.

133 1835 Half Cents. Average fine. 11 pcs.

134 1853, 1855 Half Cents. Fine and very fine. 2 pcs.

135 1859 Nickel Cent. Fine proof.

136 1859 Nickel Cent. Fine proof.

137 1859 Nickel Cents. Proofs. 2 pcs.

138 1864 Nickel Cent. Proof.

139 1857, 1859, 1862. Nickel Cents. Very fine. 3 pcs.

140 1864 (1), 1879 (11). Bronze Cents. Very fine or uncirculated. 12 pcs.

141 1882 Bronze Cent. Proof.

142 1836 First Steam Coinage. Mar. 23. Copper, mint state. 18.

143 1868 Annual Assay. Peace destroying implements of war. Aluminum proof. 22.

144 1869 Columbia seated; rev., ANNUAL ASSAY, in wreath, LET US HAVE PEACE on scroll above. Bronze, mint state. 22.

145 1873 Cloaked figure resting against side of arch, with J. POLLOCK, DIRECTOR, in exergue; rev., draped mortuary altar inscribed ECKFELDT surmounted by an urn, ANNUAL ASSAY, 1873, all within a wreath of cypress. Silver proof.

146 1652 Massachusetts Oak tree Shilling. Wyatt's copy.

147 1665 XII Pence; rev., M N. E. COL. Copper; modern.

148 1773 Virginia Halfpenny. Uncirculated.

149 1795 Bust of Washington; rev., a grate. London Halfp. token; fine.

150 Success to the United States (2); North Carolina token. Brass, fair and good, latter pierced. 3 pcs.

151 Colonial Coins. Connecticut, Vermont, New Jersey, Massachusetts, etc. Poor to good, 3 pierced. 28 pcs.

152 Rosa Americana, 1733; Confederatio; God preserve Carolina, etc. Electros of rare Colonials. 9 pcs.

153 Jacksonian or Hard Times Tokens, and early Store Cards. All different, as described by Haseltine, Proskey, Low and Scott. Good to very fine. 50 pcs.

154 Same. All different. Fair to fine. 30 pcs.

155 Another lot. 28 varieties. Fair to fine. 50 pcs.

156 Another lot. 25 varieties. Fair to fine. 50 pcs.

157 Another lot. 21 varieties. Fair to fine. 50 pcs.

158 Balance of the collection ; over 20 varieties. Poor to fine, a few pierced. 159 pcs.

159 Bust of Washington in dotted oval, counterstamped on old English Halfpenny. Good ; *rare.*

160 U. S., First Steam Coinage, 1836 ; Jacksonian tokens, etc., all size of the old Cent. Poor to fine. 3 pierced. 17 pcs.

161 1837 Feuchtwanger Cents. Good and fine. 4 pcs.

162 Copperheads or War Tokens. Silver, several struck over U. S. Dimes. Fine and *rare.* 1[illegible] pcs.

163 Copperheads or War Tokens. Poor to fine, a few pierced, four sutlers' tokens included. 130 pcs.

U. S. MEDALS, STORE CARDS, ETC.

164 1756 Arms of Philadelphia ; rev., burning village, KITTANING DESTROYED. Bronze, very fine early impression before the dies broke. 30.

165 George Washington. Old bust right, GEORGE WASHINGTON, BORN FEBRUARY 11, 1732, DIED DECEMBER 21, 1799 : rev., Fame flying over land and sea, WISDOM, VIRTUE & PATRIOTISM, 1803. Bronze, fine, a very *rare* and valuable medal. 25.

166 Washington on horseback ; rev., CARRY ME TO ATWOOD, etc. Brass, poor but everything legible. *Rare.* 16.

167 Bust to left, WASHINGTON ; rev., HE LIVED FOR HIS COUNTRY in wreath. Copper proof. 18.

168 Same obv. ; rev., MADE FROM COPPER TAKEN FROM THE RUINS OF THE TURPENTINE WORKS, NEWBERN N. C. DESTROYED BY THE REBELS MARCH 14 1862. Copper proof. *Rare.* 18.

169 Same bust, THE FATHER OF OUR COUNTRY ; rev., as in 167. Copper proof. 18.

170 Bust of Washington r. ; rev., 13 stars. Copper proof. 9½.

171 Bust of Jackson, OLD HICKORY ; rev., inscription in 14 lines. Copper proof. 22.

172 Bust of Harrison over semi-circle of stars ; rev., log cabin, THE HOME OF GENERAL HARRISON, etc. Copper, nearly proof. 18.

173 Bust of Henry Clay: rev., scales. Brass, uncirculated, pierced. 15. 9 pcs.

174 Bust of Lincoln three-fourths r.; ABRAHAM LINCOLN, BORN FEB. 12. 1809; rev., MADE FROM COPPER, etc., as in 168. Copper proof, *rare*. 18.

175 Bust of Lincoln; rev., MARTYR TO LIBERTY. Oval, bronze, very fine. 16.

176 Head of Lincoln in circle of stars; rev., FREEDOM, JUSTICE, TRUTH. Copper, silvered, pierced. Smallest Lincoln medal. 9.

177 Stephen A. Douglas, Grant, Garfield, Hancock. Copper and brass, average very fine, one pierced. 12 to 18. 9 pcs.

178 Geo. B. McClellan. Bust to left, WAR OF 1861; rev., blank, for inscription of soldier's name, company and regt; intended for identification in case of death on battlefield. Brass proof, pierced. 20. 10 pcs.

179 Duplicates of last. 10 pcs.

180 Same as last. 8 pcs.

181 Bust of Garfield; rev., REPUBLICAN CANDIDATE 1880 (3); bust of Hancock; rev., DEMOCRATIC CANDIDATE 1880 (3); Copper proof. 15. 6 pcs.

182 Continental seals. Perseverando, etc. Four varieties; very fine. Copper (2) and W. M. 25. 5 pcs.

183 Arms of Philadelphia; rev., TESTIMONIAL TO CAPTAINS CREIGHTON, LOW, STOUFFER, etc., 1854. Bronze, mint state. 47.

184 Brass and W.m. Calendars. Several varieties, of which two with Washington on horseback. Fair to fine. 22 to 25. 14 pcs.

185 Libertas Americana; rev., bust of Washington. Silver, thick planchet, very fine. 16.

186 Copy of the New England Elephant piece. Silver, proof. 18.

187 Boston Numismatic Society. Copper and brass, nearly proof. 20. 2 pcs.

188 Eagle, UNITED STATES OF AMERICA; rev., EXPLORING EXPEDITION, U. S. SHIP . . . Tin, pierced, fine, scarce. 16.

189 Massachusetts for justice; Success to Republican Principles. Tin and brass; fine. 16 and 18. 4 pcs.

190 Eagle, MASSACHUSETTS, 1866; rev., LEXINGTON, APRIL 19, 1775, BALTIMORE APRIL 19 1861. Silver, fine. 18.

191 U. S. Armory, Springfield, Mass.; Soldier's Fair, Springfield, Mass., 1864. Copper and w.m., two with bust of Washington. Very fine and proof. 18. 8 pcs.

192 Penn's Treaty; Penn's bi-centennial, 1882, etc. Brass, fine to proof, one pierced. 9 to 20. 7 pcs.

193 Washington's headquarters at Tappan (2); Old Middle Dutch Church, Nassau St., N. Y. Copper and w.m., fine. 20 and 22. 3 pcs.

194 J. A. Bolen. Four with bust; several combinations of dies. Copper, brass and w.m. Fine to proof. 16 to 18. 7 pcs.

195 James E. Wolff, Petersburg, Va. Hat; rev., a wolf. Brass and german silver. Nearly proof. 16. 10 pcs.

196 Same as last. 10 pcs.

197 Same as last. 12 pcs.

198 25th Anniversary, Phila. Rifle Club, 1871. Brass, nearly proof. 14 pcs.

199 Woodgate & Co., importers of brandies, etc., New York, 1860; rev., American shield surrounded by 13 stars. REPRESENTED BY J. N. T. LEVICK. Copper proof, *rare*. 18.

200 Duplicates of last. Same condition. 2 pcs.

201 Same as last. Rarely offered. 3 pcs.

202 Bust of Apollo; rev., Apollo gardens, "Made from copper taken from the ruins of Turpentine Works, Newbern, N. C., etc." All different, *rare*. Copper, proof. 18. 6 pcs.

203 Duplicates of last. All different. Copper proof. 5 pcs.

204 Busts of Washington, Lincoln, Webster, De Forest, Apollo, with various combinations of reverse dies, W.m., nearly proof, no duplicates. 18. 19 pcs.

205 Duplicates, 11 varieties. 19 pcs.

206 H. Mulligan, Phila.; N.C. Folger, N.O.; Browning Bros., Druggists, Phila.; Rickey's Book Store, Dayton, O.; Benj. F. Fotterall, Vicksburg; C. W. Jackson; W. A. Drown & Co., etc. Copper and brass, nearly all proof. Duplicates. 18 to 20. 68 pcs.

207 Medals, Store Cards. W.m., fine lot. 12 to 25. 35 pcs.

208 Dr. J. G. Hewett, "bone setter," etc., New York. Scarce medical. Copper, fine. 18.

209 P. Evans, Cincinnati; Farnsworth, Phipps & Co., Boston; E. L. Percy, Troy, N. Y.; H. Law, baker, New York. Scarce Store Cards. Composition metal (1), copper. 17 and 18. 4 pcs.

210 Peale's Museum, Philadelphia; "Admit," etc. Copper, fine. 21.

211 Edward Everett (var.); "Par Nobile Fratrum"; Balto. Monument; Joannes Allan, Antiquary; Gen'l Peter Lyne; Mobile Jockey Club, etc. Copper, only one duplicate, very fine. 18 to 22. 10 pcs.

212 David M. Lyle; Stephen Girard; Kossuth; Green & Wetmore, etc. Medalets and Store Cards. Brass, good and fine. 12 to 24. 16 pcs.

213 Joannes Allan; Kossuth; R. Lovett, Jr.; W. W. Wilbur, Charleston, S. C., etc. Copper, brass, and w.m., good to fine, 3 pierced. 9 to 20. 26 pcs.

214 Randall & Co., Keach, Benj. Jury, Nonpareil, Baltimore; Garrett Townsend, George Bruchlacher, A. Weber, Louisville; P. Evans, Cin., O. Silver, german silver and nickel. Half Dime size to 16. Good and fine, scarce. 10 pcs.

215 Jetons, Spiel-Marks, Omnibus Tokens, etc. Brass, very fine. 10 to 22. 35 pcs.

216 Similar lot. Fair to very good; brass and w.m., three pierced. 20 pcs.

217 Hand holding dagger surmounted by cap, LIBERTY. AND. EQUALITY; rev., blank. Brass, good, possibly of the Revolutionary period. 15.

218 Portrait of Ellsworth; rev., portrait of Brownell, the Avenger. Encased ferrotype. Very scarce. 2 pcs.

219 Bust of John Brown; rev., a gibbet, 1859. Brass, fine. 20.

220 Bust of Gen. Jas. A. Beaver; rev., a pair of crutches THE ONLY MEDAL HE WEARS. Bronze proof. 16.

221 Peace Celebration by the German-Americans, San Francisco, 1871. Fine, silver (?). 19.

222 1775–1875. Centennial of the Mecklenburg Declaration of Independence. Hands joined, and branch bearing wasp's nest and Liberty cap. Copper, very fine. 19.

223 1875 Bunker Hill Centennial, one commemorative of the visit of the 7th Regt., N. Y. N. G. to Boston. Brass (pierced) and copper. Very fine. 17 and 20. 2 pcs.

224 1876 Hundredth Anniversary of American Independence. Liberty with glaive, under radiant stars; rev., inscription. The official medal; silver, very fine. 24.

225 Duplicate. Silver, fine.

226 Another; bronze, mint state.

227 1876 Independence Hall; rev., Liberty bell (16); Centennial Art Gallery (2); "Washington, fit keystone," etc. W.m. 14 to 26. 21 pcs.

228 1876 Memorial Medalet (2); the Lord's Prayer (3). Struck within Int. Exch. building. Silver (1,) brass, pierced. 14 and 16. 5 pcs.

229 1876 Lowell Centennial. Female seated, spinning; rev., monogram. W.m., silvered, a few gilt, pierced, very fine. 16. 38 pcs.

230 1876 Centennial Reception, Ball, and Tea-party, Academy of Music, N. Y. Bust of Washington; rev., bust of Martha W. Copper, mint state. 17. 2 pcs.

231 1876 Women's Pavillion, Phila. *Porcelain.* 34.

232 Saratoga Monument Association. Cop., mint state. 22.

233 1878 Centennial of the battle and massacre of Wyoming. A fine medal, bronze, mint state. 24.

234 1881 Centennial of Groton Heights, and burning of New London. W.m., fine. 25.

235 1881 13th Regt. N. Y. N. G. to Yorktown. Brass, mint state. 18. 2 pcs.

236 1887 Centennial of first settlement, Seneca Falls, N. Y. W.m., pierced, with pin, fine and scarce. 25. 2 pcs.

237 Duplicates of last. 3 pcs.

238 1880 Armory Fair, Scranton City Guard. Copper proof. 18. 3 pcs.

239 1881 Armory Fair, 9th Regt., N. J. N. G. W.m. proof. 18. 3 pcs.

240 Exposition Medals. Cincinnati, 1870, 1872, 1873; Pittsburg, 1878, 1879; Chicago, 1875; Louisville, 1883; National Peace Jubilee, Boston, 1869. Brass (2), w.m. No duplicates, very fine, four pierced. 17 to 24. 9 pcs.

241 Duplicates of last; Brooklyn Bridge; Pioneer Base Ball Club; John Wesley Sabbath School, etc. W.m., two brass, seven pierced. 17 to 23. 15 pcs.

242 1865 Grand Parade Phila. Firemen. W.m. proof. 32.

243 1840 Albany Catholic Total Abstinence Society. W.m., very fine. 29.

244 Pius IX, 1877, Golden Jubilee; St. Patrick's Cathedral, etc. Bronze (1), and w.m., fine, 2 pierced. 18 to 22. 6 pcs.

245 Agr. and Hort. Exh., Sacramento, Cal.; Ohio State Board of Agriculture. W.m., fine. 24 and 32. 2 pcs.

246 Masonic Medal. Bust l. within square and compasses; rev., grand magic square. W.m. proof. 32.

247 Masonic Temple, Phila.; New Masonic Hall, Phila.; Masonic Temple, Boston; bust of Lafayette, rev. square and compasses; Egyptian Obelisk; Hollandsche Loge, Staat van Niew York; John Thornley, Phila. Brass (1), w.m. (9), last named rubber. Fine and scarce lot. 13 to 24. 11 pcs.

248 Egyptian Obelisk, N. Y., 1880. Brass proof, scarce. 22.

249 W. W. Cotteral, P. M., Middletown, Ind.; W. K. Lanphear, Cincinnati, O. Masonic War Tokens. Brass and copper, uncirculated, *rare*. 2 pcs.

250 Odd Fellows, 31st anniversary, 1876; Ninth Precinct House, Phila. W.m. and copper, uncirculated. 14. 3 pcs.

251 Engraved Dime, incuse impression of American eagle on copper planchet; Seal; Odds and Ends. 30 pcs.

252 Capture of Stony Point; "Our Flag trampled upon," etc. Electros, shells and casts, several of rare medals. Large and small; good lot. 28 pcs.

253 Sixth Corps Badge; head of Columbia; Pins, Models, trial impression of heads, etc. A curious lot. 20 pcs.

254 Engraved silver Disk, for rescue from drowning. 30.

255 Eagle on shield, labels inscribed "Thomas Deacon;" Wilmington, Del.; rev., "Stove, tin, sheet iron," etc. Curious Store Card. Silver. 16.

256 Rubber, leather, wood, and metallic Shell Medals and Store Cards. 14 pcs.

256a Spanish Real of 1776, counterstamped with Liberty cap in radiant rays, between which thirty stars, 1 DOLLAR beneath. In good condition, of unknown origin, the only other specimen I ever saw sold as an American coin of necessity for $5.00.

256b Bust of Archimedes, N. ENGLAND SOC. FOR PROMOTION OF MANUFACTURES AND MECHANIC ARTS, 1826 ; rev., emblematic of progress in mechanical arts, ARCHIMEDES, GALILEO, NEWTON, FRANKLIN, WATT, FULTON, label beneath, engraved FRANCIS PEABODY. Fine and rare silver medal by *Gobrecht*. 45.

FOREIGN COINS AND MEDALS; SILVER.

257 Bavaria. Max. Joseph. 1765. Crown. Good.

258 Bavaria. Visit of Louis Ch. Augustus to French mint, 1806. Bust; rev., inscription. Very fine. 18.

259 Maximilian Joseph. 1824. Jubilee medalet, and another. Very fine. 10. 2 pcs.

260 Brazil. 1859–1866. 200, 500, 1000 Reis. Uncirculated. 3 pcs.

261 England. Henry III, Sithric III (Ireland). Pennies; one pierced, one badly broken on edge; good to fine. 4 pcs.

262 Charles II, 1673, 2d.; Anne, 1708, Shilling; George II, 1739, Penny, 1746, 2d. ; William IV, 1832, 4d., 1834, 3d. ; Victoria, 1883, 6d. (2) Good to uncirculated. 8 pcs.

263 Star of the Garter; rev., VITTORIA AND LEIPZIG in wreath. Rare military medal, good. 19.

264 France. Louis IX (1270). The gate of Tours; rev., short cross. Fair. 2 pcs.

265 1750 Louis XV. Crown. Fair, gilt.

266 Germany. Friendship and religious medals. Very fine. 19 and 24. 2 pcs.

267 1872 Guatemala. Peso or Dollar. Fine.

268 1883 Hawaii. Kalakaua I. Dimes. Uncir. 6 pcs.

269 India. Rupees, native inscription. Very good. 2 pcs.

270 Lisbon. Medal struck in Germany on the destruction of the city by earthquake, and its rebuilding. Father Time pointing to distant city, 1755 in the field ; rev., Youth pointing to blooming plant. Fine and scarce. 20.

271 Another medal on the same subject. Allegorical group of female figures. POST FATA RESURGENS; rev., equestrian statue of Joseph I, MAGNANIMO RESTITUTORI. Fine, a *rare* medal. 30.

272 1848 Mexico. Dollar. Very good.

273 1781 Netherlands. Four shields linked, GEWAPENDE NEUTRALITEIT; rev., IEHOVAH, etc., in 10 lines. Fine and scarce medal. 20.

274 1782 Netherlands. Female figure with Liberty cap on staff and Mercury's wand, NEDERLAND VERKLAARD AMERICA VRY; rev., trophy of bales of merchandise and flags, DE ALGEMEENE WENSCH. Fine and scarce medal; like the last described, relates to the United States. 22.

275 1750 Russia. Elizabeth. Rouble. Fair.

276 1756 Ratisbon. Crown. Bust of Francis and view of the city. Good, gilt.

277 1836 Socabaya. Eagle with laurel branch, DE LA PAZ AL PERU; rev., EN SOCABAYA A. 7. DE FEBRERO 1836. Oval, with loop. Fine, *rare*. 20.

278 Scotland. Bust of Mary Stuart, MARIA D. G. ANG. SCO. FR. ET HI. REGINA; rev., female seated upon a rock, O. DEA. CERTE. Fair, *rare*. 21.

279 1673 Salzburg. Square $\frac{1}{8}$ Thaler. Good, one pierced on edge. 2 pcs.

280 1854 Sicily. Ferdinand II. Crown. Very fine.

281 1684 Charles II, King of Spain and Naples, Crown, rev., two worlds crowned; another, 1791, Ferdinand IV and M. Carolina, Crown, rev., globe under radiant sun. Poor and fair. 2 pcs.

282 Sweden. Bust of Gustavus Adolphus; rev., crowned monogram. Has been gilt, fine. 15.

283 Brunswick, Denmark, France, India, German States, Papal States, Russia, Sicily, etc. Coins and Medalets; fine lot, of which several deserve special descriptions. 10 to 19. 17 pcs.

284 Turkey and dependencies. Interesting lot for Arabic scholar. Many old, silver and base, good to fine, six pierced. 8 to 24. 39 pcs.

285 Silver and base Coins. Lot includes several mediaeval grossus and pennies, Cob money, Half Dollar of Maximilian, Ragusa Half Crown, etc. An excellent lot from which to make selections. Average condition good, five pierced. 123 pcs.

286 Military Medal. Rose in tressure; rev., a crown, ICH KAEMPFE FUER DAS RECHT. Copper gilt, with ring.

287 Pascal, Jean Claude, Prince Albert, Dutch Jetons, Liberia Colonization Society, a few nickel coins. Bronze, brass, etc., average fine. 10 to 28. 16 pcs.

The following are Ancient.

288 Ilium, Larissa, Metapontum, Paestum, Perga, Venusia, etc. Greek coins. Bronze, fair to fine. 9 to 14. 11 pcs.

289 Maronea, Neapolis, Campania, and Macedonia. Silver, fair, one pierced. 9 and 10. 3 pcs.

290 Magnesia, Ionia. Bearded head; rev., naked figure of Apollo and inscription. ~~A beautiful~~ Tetradrachm, but ~~pronounced to be~~ modern.

291 Greek Coins, silver (4); Rome, bronze, modern. 5 pcs.

292 Head facing: rev., dog sleeping, ATR. Bronze Aes. Size 48. Fine, modern.

293 Persia. Sapor II. Silver Drachm, very good, crack on edge.

294 Aes, reduced size: Germanicus. Vespasian, M. Aurelius, Anastasius. Constantinus X, Romanus II, Carausius, emperor in Britain, etc. G, M, and T. B. Poor to good. 15 pcs.

295 Miscellaneous silver Denarii. Poor to good. 8 pcs.

296 Fractional Currency. 3 Cents, bust of Washington, light shading behind head. New.

297 25 Cents. Bust of Fessenden. green back. New.

298 Autographic signatures of members of Congress, S. S. Cox, Warner Miller, Hiscock, Merrill; also Hancock, Fitz John Porter, Nast, etc. 17 pcs.

299 S. K. Harzfeld. Coin Sale Catalogues, Different. 5 pcs.

A FEW GOLD COINS.

300 England. George II. 1739. Double Guinea. Bust to left; rev., crowned shield. Fine, *rare*.

301 United States. 1849. Mormon $5.00. Mitre over eye, TO THE LORD HOLINESS; rev., hands joined. Very good, *rare*.

302 California Half and Quarter Dollars. Both pierced. 2 pcs.

303 1878 Three Dollars. Fine.
304 1849 Dollar. Very good.
305 1856 Dollar. Nearly fine.
306 1857 Dollar. Nearly fine.
307 1861 Dollar. Very good.
308 1862 Dollar. Nearly fine.

UNITED STATES COINS.

309 1864 Proof set. One, Half, Quarter Dollars, Dime and Half Dime, Three Cents, 2 and 1 Cents bronze, One Cent nickel. Fine and *rare*. 9 pcs.
310 1865 Complete Set. Fine proofs. 9 pcs.
311 1866 Complete Set. Fine proofs. 10 pcs.
312 1871 Complete Set. Fine proofs. 10 pcs.
313 1872 Complete Set. Fine proofs. 10 pcs.
314 1873 Without arrows. Somewhat discolored. 10 pcs.
315 1878 Minor Proof Set. 3 pcs.
316 1856 Nickel Cent. Fine proof, *rare*.
317 1856 Nickel Cent. Proof, *rare*.
318 1858 Nickel Cent. Small eagle; rev., oak wreath. Proof.
319 1868 5, 3, 1 Cents; rev., numerals in wreath. Fine proofs, *rare* set. 3 pcs.
320 1795 Dollar. Flowing hair. Sharp, perfect impression; an extremely fine dollar. *Rare*.
321 1796 Dollar. Small pin-marks, fine.
322 1797 Dollar. Seven stars facing. Fine, scarce.
323 1798 Dollar. Close date; good.
324 1799 Dollar. Very fair.
325 1801 Dollar. Very good.
326 1802 Dollar, recut date. Nearly fine.
327 1836 Dollar. Flying eagle. Fine.
328 1842 Dollar. Very good.
329 1846 Dollar, *Orleans m*. Nearly fine.
330 1859 Dollar, *Orleans m*. Very good.
331 1860 Dollar, *Orleans m*. Fine.
332 1860 Dollar, *Orleans m*. Fine.
333 1866 Dollar. Hay-marked proof.

334 1867 Dollar. Very good.

335 1873 Dollar, *Carson City m.* Good.

336 1794 Half Dollar. Considerably circulated, but everything plain. Scarce.

337 1795 Half Dollars. Fair and good. 2 pcs.

338 1796 Half Dollar, 16 stars. Fine. An extremely desirable specimen of this very rare date.

339 1801 Half Dollar. Plugged through date. Good.

340 1802 Half Dollar. A cut through head and date. Very good, scarce.

341 1803 Half Dollar. Very good.

342 1805 Half Dollar. Very good.

343 1806 Half Dollar. Pointed 6 fine.

344 1808 Half Dollar. Fair.

345 1815 Half Dollar. Good, *rare.*

346 1817 Half Dollar. Fine.

347 1818 Half Dollar. Fine.

348 1823, 1831 Half Dollars. Good. 2 pcs.

349 1839 Half Dollar. Bust of Liberty. Fine.

350 1844 Half Dollar, *Orleans m.* Good.

351 1851 Half Dollar, *Orleans m.* Very good, nicked.

352 1852 Half Dollar, *Orleans m.* Very good, *rare.*

353 1852 Half Dollar, *Orleans m.* Good, *rare.*

354 1853 Half Dollar, *Orleans m.* Arrows removed. Very fair.

355 1856 Half Dollar, *Orleans m.* Fine.

356 1858 Half Dollar, *Orleans m.* Very good.

357 1859 Half Dollar, *Orleans m.* Fine.

358 1859 Half Dollar, *Orleans m.* Fine.

359 1866 Half Dollar, *San Fr. m.*, without motto. Good.

360 1875 Half Dollar, *San Fr. m.* Fine.

361 1876 Half Dollar, *San Fr. m.* Fine.

362 1876 Half Dollar. Fair.

363 1876 Half Dollar, *C. City m.* Fine.

364 1877 Half Dollar, *San Fr. m.* Uncirculated.

365 1877 Half Dollars, duplicates of last. Uncir. 2 pcs.

366 1883 Half Dollar. Very good.

367 1806, 1807, 1818. Quarter Dollars. Poor, one pierced. 3 pcs.

368 1828 Quarter Dollar. Struck on brilliant planchet, sharp, uncirculated. *Rare* and desirable.

369 1834, 1835, 1837. Quarter Dollars. Very good. 3 pcs.

370 1840, 1846, 1850. Quarter Dollars, former and last *O. m.* Good to fine. 3 pcs.

371 1853 Quarter Dollars, with and without (removed) arrows, *P. and O. m.* Very good. 2 pcs.

372 1856, 1858, 1861. Quarter Dollars. Good to fine. 3 pcs.

373 1869, 1873. Quarter Dollars. Former *San Fr. m*, latter without arrows. Very good. 2 pcs.

374 1877 Quarter Dollars. *C. City and San Fr. m.* Uncirculated. 2 pcs.

375 1877 Quarter Dollars. Same mints, uncir. 2 pcs.

376 1878 Quarter Dollar. Uncirculated.

377 1878 Quarter Dollars. *C. City m.* Uncir. 2 pcs.

378 1882, 1888 (*San Fr. m.*) Quarter Dollars. Good and fine. 2 pcs.

379 Half (1), Quarter Dollars (4), Dime (1). Engraved on one side and otherwise damaged. 6 pcs.

380 1875 Twenty Cents. Dull proof.

381 1875 Twenty Cents. Fine.

382 1796 Dime. Very fine impression; *rare.*

383 1798 over '97. Dime. Very fair, scarce.

384 1803 Dime. Good, *rare.*

385 1805 Dime. Very fair, everything plain.

386 1807 Dime. Good.

387 1814, 1820. Dimes. Good. 2 pcs.

388 1821 Dime. Small date. Brilliant, sharp and uncirc.; *rare.* The specimen in the Davis sale sold for $4.

389 1821 Dime. Large date. Very good.

390 1823, 1824, over '22. Dimes. Fair. 2 pcs.

391 1825, 1827, 1828 (sm. date). Dimes. Very fair. 3 pcs.

392 1830–1837 (var.). Dimes, consecutive. Good. 9 pcs.

393 1837 Dime. Liberty seated: uncirculated.

394 1838–1845. Dimes, consecutive. Very good. 8 pcs.

395 1846 Dime. Good, scarce.

396 1846 Dime. Good, scarce.

397 1847–1859. Dimes, consecutive, with varieties of mint, etc. Average very good. 16 pcs.

398 1860 Dimes. *Phila. and San Fr. m.* (stars). Fine and fair. 2 pcs.

399 1861–1883. Dimes, consecutive, varieties of mints, etc. Very good to fine. 24 pcs.

400 1884–1889. Dimes, consecutive; uncirculated. 9 pcs.

401 1888 Dime. Proof.

402 1794 Half Dime. Very good, *rare.*

403 1795 Half Dime. Very fair; bent.

404 1796 Half Dime. Very fine, *rare* and desirable.

405. 1797 Half Dime. 15 stars. Fine, centre of rev. very weak, *rare.*

406 1803 Half Dime. Obv. very good, rev. fair. *Rare.*

407 1834–1861. Half Dimes. Fair to very good. 11 pcs.

408 Three Cents. 1851–1854, '56, '57, '59, '60, '61, '62. Poor to fine. 16 pcs.

409 Five Cents Nickel. 1866, '67 (2 var.), '68–'76, '79, '81–'89. Early dates very good, later uncir. 27 pcs.

410 Three Cents Nickel. 1865–'70, '71–'76, '81. Good to fine. 20 pcs.

411 1793 Chain Cent. Obv. rather poor, rev. fair. Scarce.

412 1809 Cent. Good, scarce.

413 1809 Cent. Rather poor.

414 1813 Cent. Good.

415 1818, '28 (3) Cents. Very good. 4 pcs.

416 1857 Cent. Small date. Proof.

417 1794 Half Cent. Date distant from bust. Very good, *rare.*

418 1805 Half Cent; rev., stemless wreath. Fine.

419 1806 Half Cents, with and without stems to wreath. Fine. 2 pcs.

420 1811 Half Cent. Date plain: poor, scarce.

421 1833, '34, 35. Half Cents. Very fine and uncir. 3 pcs.

422 1849 Half Cent. Small date; proof obverse, *rare.*

423 1851, '53, '55. Half Cents. Fine. 3 pcs.

424 1852 Half Cent. Proof obv., *rare.*

425 1804–'51. Half Cents. 9 poor, 2 fine, 4 pierced. 11 pcs.

426 1857–'88. Nickel and bronze Cents. Nearly all uncirculated; duplicates. 17 pcs.

427 1652 Pine tree VI and IIId., Oak tree IId., Wyatt's copies. Fine, deceptive. 3 pcs.

428 1783 Chalmers' Annapolis Shilling. Very good, slightly clipped on edge, scarce.

429 1783 Chalmers' Threepence. Hands clasped; rev., shrub in wreath. Fine, *rare.*

430 1722 Rosa Americana. Penny. Bust of George I; rev., blooming rose. Struck in brass; very good, *rare.*

430*a* 1723 Rosa Americana. Penny; rev., crowned rose. Brass; very good, *rare.*

431 1773 Virginia Halfpence. Fine impression; uncir.

432 U. S. A. or Bar Cent. Sharp; uncirculated.

433 1794 Talbot, Allum & Lee. N. Y. Cent. Fine impression; uncirculated.

434 1794 Same as last, but from different reverse die. Struck in *brass*; fine and *rare.*

435 1795 Cent, issued by the same firm. Very fine.

436 Electros of Higley coppers, etc. 5 pcs.

437 1783 Georgius Triumpho. Cent. Very fair.

438 1783 Washington and Independence; rev., "Unity States." Fine.

439 1783 Washington and Independence. Draped bust; rev., "United States." Recent impression from original dies. Uncirculated. 2 pcs.

440 1791 Washington Cent; large eagle rev. Good.

441 1791 Washington Cent; small eagle rev. Uncirculated.

442 Military bust to l., GEORGE WASHINGTON; rev., American shield, LIBERTY AND SECURITY; edge inscribed AN ASYLUM, etc. Very fine impression, desirable specimen.

443 Same as last, but struck in brass. Fine, pierced above head.

444 1792 Washington Half Dollar. Silver, uncirculated; *copy* beneath eagle.

445 Bust of Washington; rev., bust of Lafayette, 1824. Silver, obv. and rev. soldered together. 9.

446 George Washington. Bust; rev., "Cabinet of Medals, U. S. Mint." Bronze, very fine. 38.

447 Bust of Washington. Oath of Allegiance medal. Bronze, very fine. 19.

448 Bust of Washington; rev., "Great Central Fair;" bust of Grant; rev., "General U. S. Grant." Silver medalets, uncir. and proof, latter pierced. 12. 2 pcs.

449 Ships, Colonies and Commerce; Jacksonian tokens; Feuchtwanger Cent; Gov. Wm. H. Seward, etc. Copper and brass; very good and fine, one pierced. 13 pcs.

450 1876 Phila. Exposition. Bust of Liberty; rev., "Centennial Anniversary," etc. Brass and german silver, proof. 15. 2 pcs.

451 Harrison Log Cabin; Rough and Ready. Brass buttons of Political Campaigns. 3 pcs.

452 1882 Agr. Soc. of So. Carolina; rev., name engraved. Silver, very fine. 24.

453 Gen. T. J. Jackson (Stonewall). Bust; rev., names of battles. Tin, fine. 32.

454 "No Submission to the North;" rev., "The wealth of the South," shield; forming three combinations of dies. Copper and w.m., very fine. 14. 5 pcs.

455 St. Louis. 1878, Fair and Exposition; 1884, Exp. and Music Hall; 1884, 1st Nat. Conv. of Cattle men; 1885, Cattle Fair; 1887, Exp. and Music Hall. W.m., 4 pierced, one with pin. 19 to 32. 5 pcs.

456 State of Missouri. "Half Dime"; rev., scales, "Good at Nicholson's." German silver, very good and *rare*.

457 American eagle with wings expanded and facing left, grasps an olive branch on American shield, ST LOUIS POST OFFICE above; rev., blank, name *Frank Lapere* engraved. Copper, very fine and *rare*, interesting alike to Postage Stamp and Coin Collectors. 18.

458 Duplicate; name *C. C. Thompson* engraved on reverse. Very good.

459 American shield in trophy of flags, eagle above, ST LOUIS POST OFFICE; rev., *Lepere & Richards* engraved. W.m., pierced, very fine and *rare*. 16.

460 Same, another name engraved on rev. W.m., pierced, good and *very rare*.

461 Duplicate, another name on rev. W.m., good, pierced. 16.

462 1862 Bust of Liberty; rev., "Drover's Hotel St. Louis." War token; copper, very fine.

463 1876 Lib. Americana and two other Centennial medalets; rev., "Joel Swope's St. Louis." W.m., good and fine. 14. 3 pcs.

464 U. S. Shield, "Washington Garden and Hall by Frank Boehen & Co."; rev., "Good for 5 cents." W.m., good, *rare*. 12.

465 U. S. Cent of 1851, counterstamped "G. Deagle, 82 Pine St.," on rev. Fine.

466 "Fourth St. Opera House, St. Louis, Mo., J. S. Edwards, prop.;" rev., 5 CENTS in semi-circle of 9 stars. Brass, octagonal, fine. 18.

467 Eagle. J. & W. Van Deventer, St. Louis. Copper and german silver, fine. 18. 2 pcs.

468 A hat, "M. Harris, 502 Franklin Ave.:" rev., "Save $1 on a fine hat." Tin, uncir., fine. 19.

469 1836. "Huckel, Burrows & Jennings;" rev., "Boat stores and ship chandlery, Main St., St. Louis." Brass, nickel, fine and *rare*. 18.

470 Blank oval in American shield: rev., E JACCARD & CO., ST. LOUIS, MO. Copper, brass, german silver, w.m., one with number counterstamped in oval. Uncirculated, *rare*. 18. 5 pcs.

471 Bust of Liberty; rev., eagle, "E. Long's Dagguerian Gallery, St. Louis, Mo." Copper and brass; good and uncirculated. 18. 3 pcs.

472 1850 Eagle "Fitzgibbon daguerreotype gallery, St. Louis, Mo." Copper and silvered, very fine. 18. 3 pcs.

473 Arm grasping hammer over anvil "J. S. Pease & Co., St. Louis." Brass, nicked, good, *rare*. 17.

474 "St. Bernard Dollar Store:" "C. G. Sanders, Wood, Coal, etc., St. Louis. W.m., fine and good. 17. 2 pcs.

475 "H. Prouhet, No. 9 North 4th Street, St. Louis. Mo.;" rev., blank. Copper, fine, pierced, *rare*. 20.

476 F. L. Schmidt, Woodman Saloon, Aug. Tremann, Geo. Wolbrecht's Tivoli, Case & Co., etc. Bier and other tokens, St. Louis. Brass and nickel, very good lot for collector of local cards. 10 to 15. 13 pcs.

477 St. Louis Tokens. Engraved, counterstamped, etc. Copper, brass and lead, good, 2 pierced. 16 to 20. 7 pcs.

478 J. B. Wilson. Dime and Half Dime bread tokens. W.m., uncirculated. 10 and 12. 4 pcs.

479 Engraved medal with Masonic emblems. Silver. 24.

480 CONTINENTAL CURRENCY. Phila., 1775, May 10, $3; 1776, May 9, $2, 4; July 22, $3, 30: Nov. 2, $4, 8; 1777, Feb. 26, $4, 8: May 20, $30 (2). Good. 11 notes.

481 Phila., 1778, Sept. 26, $8, 30 (8). First fair, balance very fine. 9 notes.

482 Yorktown, 1778, April 11, $4, 30. Good and fine, scarce. 2 notes.

483 Virginia, 1776, Oct. 7, $8, 10. Thick paper, good. 2 notes.

484 POSTAGE CURRENCY, 5, 10, 25, 50 Cents; *A. B. Co.* Cut edges, 25c., considerably circulated, others fine. 4 notes.

485 5, 10, 25, 50c. Same; good to fine. 4 notes.

486 5 (3), 10, 50c. Same: good to fine. 5 notes.

487 5 Cents. Same issue, without monog., perforated edges. Very fine; *rare.*

488 FRACTIONAL CURRENCY, 3 Cents. Bust of Washington in oval; good to fine, scarce. 3 notes.

489 10c. Bust of Washington in oval, gold numbers at corners. Fine. 3 notes.

490 5, 10, 25, 50c. Bust of Washington in gold oval. Fine. 4 notes.

491 5, 10, 25, 50c. Duplicate set, fine. 4 notes.

492 5, 10 Cents. Same issue, fine. 2 notes.

493 5 Cents. Bust of Clark. Fine. 4 notes.

494 25 Cents. Bust of Fessenden. *Red back*, very fine and *rare.*

495 25 Cents. Same, green back. Fine. 2 notes.

496 50 Cents. Bust and autographic signatures of Spinner & Colby; *red back.* Considerably circulated, *rare.*

497 50 Cents. Same (2); Liberty seated. Green backs, fine. 3 notes.

498 25 Cents. Bust of Washington at left side. Good to very fine. 4 notes.

499 50 Cents. Bust of Lincoln. Fine, *rare.*

500 25 Cents. Bust of Walker. Good to very fine. 5 notes.

501 15 Cents. Bust of Lib. at left. Fine. 3 notes.

502 10 Cents. Bust of Lib. at left. Fine. 3 notes.

503 10 Cents. Bust of Meredith, red seal. Fine. 4 notes.

504 50 Cents. Bust of Crawford. New, crisp.

505 50 Cents. Duplicate; fine.

506 50 Cents. Same. Good and very good. 2 notes.

FOREIGN COINS; SILVER.

507 Austria. 1846, 1855. 20 and 10 Kr. Fine and uncir. 2 pcs.

508 1860 Francis Joseph. Florin; fine.

509 1877 Same. Florin for Hungary. Very fine.

510 Baden. Leopold, 1852. ½ Gulden. Fine.

511 Bavaria. Max. Joseph, 1771. Thaler; fair.

512 Bolivia. 1830, 1846. Half and One Peso or Dollar. Good. 2 pcs.

513 Brazil. Pedro II, 1857. 1000 Reis. Fine.

514 Brunswick Luneburg. John Frederic, 1679. ⅓ Medallic Thaler. Bust r.; rev., palm tree on island, ship sailing at each side. Fine, *rare*.

515 Canada. 1858. 20 Cents. Fine.

516 1870 25, 50 Cents. Uncirculated. 2 pcs.

517 1870 25, 50 Cents. Uncirculated. 2 pcs.

518 1871 50 Cents. Good.

519 Central America. 1836. Dollar. Sun rising over mountains; rev., tree. Fine.

520 Chili. 1853, 1856. Half and 1 Peso or Dollar. Good and fine. 2 pcs.

521 Colombia. 1866. Peso or Dollar. Fine.

522 England. Silver Pennies of Edward and Henry, Sixpence of Elizabeth, 2d. of Chas. II. Poor to fair. two pierced. 6 pcs.

523 1723 George. Shilling, South Sea Co. Fair.

524 1787 George III. Shilling. Old bust, draped and laureate right; rev., 4 shields crosswise, a crown in the angles. 2d type; scarce, sharp, uncirculated.

525 1817 George III. Sixpence. Very good.

526 1820 George III. Pistrucci Crown. Fair only.

527 1822 Colonial Fourth Crown. Good. 2 pcs.

528 1872 Victoria. Gothic Florin. Very good.

529 1875 Victoria. Half Crown. Good.

530 Victoria. War Medal. Bust left; rev., female figure seated, BALTIC 1854–1855. Very fine, has been gilt. 24.

531 France. Napoleon III. 1867. 5 Francs. Very fine.

532 1866, '67. 1 and 2 Francs. Very good. 2 pcs.

533 1875 5 Francs. Uncirculated.

534 Guatemala. 1863. Peso or Dollar, head of Carrera. Fine.

535 Hamburg. 1876. 2 and 5 Marks. Fine. 2 pcs.

536 Hesse. Ludwig III. 1856. Gulden. Fine.

537 Italy. Victor Emanuel. 1869. 5 Lire. Fine.

538 Mexico. Maximilian. 1867. Peso or Dollar. Very good.

539 1871 50 Centavos or Half Dollar. Very good.

540 1875 Dollar, *Culiacan m.* Very fine.

541 1877 Dollar, *Zacatecas m.* Very good.

542 Prussia. Frederic William III. 1818. Thaler. Fine.

543 1855 Frederic William IV. Mansfeld Mining Thaler. Fine.

544 Peru. 1866. Sol or Dollar. Fine.

545 South Peru. 1838. Dollar. Tower and volcano at seashore; rev., radiant sun. Fine.

546 Sardinia. Charles Albert. 1841. 2 Lire. Fine.

547 Saxony. John V. 1860. Mining Thaler. Fine.

548 Switzerland. 1850. 2 Francs. Fine. 2 pcs.

549 Wurtemburg. William. 1841. Gulden for 25th anniversary of ruler. Very fair.

550 1851 William. Vereinsthaler. Fine.

551 Belgium, France, Hong Kong, Germany, Italy, Japan, Mexico, Netherlands, Peru, Papal States, Spain, Turkey. Good and fine, one pierced, half dime to two franc size. 21 pcs.

552 Cob money, Half Real and Real, base coins, etc. Fair to fine. 12 pcs.

553 Caesar Augustus. Head r., CAESAR IMP.; rev., Victory over altar, serpents at sides, ASIA (recepta). Quinarius; very good, *rare.*

554 Vespasian, Domitian, Ant. Pius, Faustina, Gordianus, Postumus. Silver Denarii, one base. Average very good. 8 pcs.

The following are copper, etc.

555 Egypt. Ptolemy. Bust of Zeus; rev., eagle. Very good.

556 Augustus, Claudius, Domitian, Nero, Maximianus, Probus, etc. Small to large bronze, poor to fine. 17 pcs.

557 Julius Caesar. Bust; rev., VENI, VIDI, VICI. G. B. Paduan, fine.

558 Napoleon I, III, Victor Emanuel, etc. Yellow bronze medalets, loop and ring. Proofs. 9 to 15. 14 pcs.

559 Paulus II (1464). Bust r.; rev., female figure, HILARITAS PUBLICA. Fine bronze medal from the Vatican mint. 28.

560 Alexander VII (1655). Bust right; rev., female figures. Fine bronze medal, pierced.

561 Papal Medalets, two with bust of Pius IX. Brass and yellow bronze, one good, two proof. 10 to 20. 3 pcs.

562 Canada. Locomotive, "Montreal & Lachine Railroad Company;" rev., a beaver, "Third class." Hole in centre for suspension. Fine, *rare*. 22.

563 England. Queen Elizabeth on horseback, ELIZABETA REG. ANG.; rev., crowned shield. Brass jeton, fine, *rare*.

564 Hawaii. 1847. Cent of Kamehameha III. Fine.

565 Copper Coins. Austria, England, East India, France, Italy, Java, Jersey, Papal States, Peru, (nickel,) Russia, Sicily, Sarawak, (pierced). A very choice lot, large and small. 29 pcs.

566 Engraved U. S. ½ Dol. (1,) Dimes (2). Odds and Ends. Fair. 16 pcs.

567 Modern Jewish Shekel. Tin, fine. 22.

567*a* Summer or Hog Isl. Shil. Brass, thick, poor; believed by owner to be authentic. A copy. 21.

568 1832 Bust of Washington in small oval; rev., "Civic procession," etc. Copper, very fine. 19.

A FEW GOLD COINS.

569 Colombia. 1837. Fourth Doubloon. Head of Liberty; rev., fasces and cornucopiae. Very good.

570 France. Louis XVI. 1786. Double Ecu d'or. Bust left; rev., crowned shields. Fine, *rare*.

571 1856 Napoleon III. 5 Francs. Fine.

572 Spain. 1786–1800. 1 (2), and 2 Dollars. Good, one pierced. 3 pcs.

573 Vienna. 1529. Siege Double Ducat. Crowned arms; rev., TYRCK. BLEGERT. WIENN DEN. XXIII. TAG SEPTEMBER ANNO. D. 1529. Square, very fine and *rare*.

574 United States. 1852. Dollar. Very fine.

575 1857 Dollar. Fine.

576 California. 1852. Half Dollar. Round, fine.

577 1853 Dollar. Octagonal; very fine, *rare*.

578 1853 Dollar. Octagonal. Variety; very good.

579 1854 Dollar. Octagonal; fine.

580 1854 Half Dollar. Round, very fine.

581 1856 Half Dollar, ~~Dollar~~. Very fine.

582 Calif. Quarter Dollar without date. Uncirculated.

583 George Washington. Bust right; rev., bust of Lincoln. Thick, brilliant proof, struck at U. S. Mint, Philadelphia. 12.

584 Bust of Lincoln, as in last described; rev., ABRAHAM LINCOLN AN HONEST MAN, THE CRISIS DEMANDS HIS RE-ELECTION 1864. Mint medalet, brilliant proof. 12.

UNITED STATES COINS.

PROOF SETS AND PATTERNS.

585 1850 One, half and quarter Dollars, Dime, half Dime, Cent. Fine proofs; *extremely rare* and desirable; not in Davis sale. 6 pcs.

586 1854 One, half and quarter Dollars, Dime, half Dime, and three Cents. Fine proofs, of *excessive rarity*, not in Davis sale. 6 pcs.

587 1857 One, half and quarter Dollars, Dime, half Dime, three Cents, copper and nickel Cents, half Cent. Fine proofs, the Dollar and half Dollar slightly stained. *Extremely rare*; a set like this in the Davis sale sold for $34. 9 pcs.

588 1858 One, half and quarter Dollars, Dime and half Dime, three Cents, Cent. Fine proofs, very slightly stained. *Extremely rare*; Davis sale, $47.50. 7 pcs.

589 1859 Same as last; fine proofs. 7 pcs.

590 1860 Perfect proofs. 7 pcs.

591 1860 Perfect proofs. 7 pcs.

592 1861 Perfect proofs. 7 pcs.

593 1862 Perfect proofs. 7 pcs.

594 1863 Perfect proofs. 7 pcs.

595 1865 One, half, quarter Dollars, Dime and half Dimes, Three Cents, silver and nickel, two and one Cents bronze. Perfect proofs. 9 pcs.

596 1865 Same as last; fine proofs. 9 pcs.

597 1866 One, half, quarter Dollars, Dime, 5 and 3 Cents silver and nickel, two (spotted) and one Cents bronze. Fine proofs. 10 pcs.

598 1866 Duplicate set. Fine proofs. 10 pcs.

599 1866 Another set. Fine proofs. 10 pcs.

600 1879 Both Dollars, half and quarter Dollars, Dime, 5 and 3 Cents nickel, one Cent bronze. Fine proofs. 8 pcs.

601 1859 Pattern Half Dollars. Head of Liberty to right; rev., HALF DOLLAR, ½ DOLLAR, 50 CENTS. Silver, all proofs, scarce. 3 pcs.

602 1859 Pattern Half Dollar. Liberty seated; rev., eagle. Silver, dull proof, scarce.

603 1859 Half Dollar. Same design; copper, dull proof.

604 1858 Pattern Nickel Cents. Large and small eagle, Indian head, combined with four revs., forming complete set of 12 varieties. Dull proofs.

DOLLARS.

605 1794 Excellent impression, the stars to left and part of rev. legend, as usual, rather weak; would be fine for date, but somewhat marred by scratches in the field and the letter E on neck. *Very rare.*

606 1795 Flowing hair. Very good.

607 1795 Fillet head. Considerably circulated; good.

608 1796 Very good; scarce.

609 1797 Six stars facing. Good; very scarce.

610 1798 Fifteen stars; rev., small eagle. Very good; *rare.*

611 1798 Large date; rev., heraldic eagle. Sharp; very fine.

612 1798 Small date; rev., heraldic eagle. Very good.

613 1799 Close date. Fair only.

614 1800 Fair only.

615 1801 T. T. counterstamped in the field. Very good.

616 1802 over '01. Rather poor.

617 1803 Stars sharp, nearly fine.

618 1836 Liberty seated, *Gobrecht* at base; rev., flying eagle and stars. Good; very scarce.

619 1838 Liberty seated; rev., flying eagle without stars, reeded edge. Sharp, beautiful, brilliant proof from the Chilton sale, March, 1865; extremely *rare*. An inferior specimen of this Dollar sold for $68 in the Davis sale.

620 1839 Same design. Fine proof; *very rare*. From same sale as last.

621 1840 Uncirculated, a few pin scratches.

622 1841 Mint lustre. Sharp, uncirculated.

623 1842 Fine; nicked.

624 1843 Very good.

625 1844 Fine.

626 1845 Fine.

627 1846 *Orleans m.* Very fine.

628 1847 Fine impression; uncirculated.

629 1848 Fine.

630 1849 Sharp impression; uncirculated.

631 1850 *Orleans m.* Very good.

632 1853 Very fine; scarce.

633 1855 A few slight pin scratches; sharp, polished planchet, an extremely fine and *rare* Dollar.

634 1856 Very fine; *rare*.

635 1857 Polished planchet; very fine, *rare*.

636 1859 *Orleans m.* Sharp impression; uncirculated.

637 1860 *Orleans m.* Sharp, uncirculated.

638 1860 *Orleans m.* Very fine; scratched.

639 1863 Very fine; needs cleaning.

640 1868 Very fine.

641 1880 *Orleans m.* Sharp, mint lustre, uncirculated.

HALF DOLLARS.

642 1794 Nick under bust; good for date, *rare.*

643 1795 Die varieties. Very fair and good. 2 pcs.

644 1796 15 stars. A fine impression, the date particularly sharp, hair a little worn in prominent parts; may be called fine, irrespective of rarity. Very desirable, extremely *rare.*

645 1797 Good for date, but plugged to right of 7. Very *rare.*

646 1801 Good; scarce.

647 1801 Fair; date plain.

648 1802 Very good; scarce.

649 1803 Fine, but nicked.

650 1803 Very good.

651 1804 Altered date; nearly fine.

652 1805 Good.

653 1806 Pointed 6. Fine.

654 1806 Pointed 6. Different dies; good and very good. 2 pcs.

655 1807 Head to right. Sharp; extremely fine.

656 1807 Head to right. Fair.

657 1807 Head to left. Extremely fine.

658 1808 over '07. Good; scarce.

659 1809 Sharp; very fine.

660 1810 Good.

661 1811 Good.

662 1812 Very good.

663 1813 Good.

664 1814 Good.

665 1815 Very good; *rare.*

666 1817 over '13. Good; scarce.

667 1817 Very good.

668 1818 over '17. Good.

669 1819 Small, wide date; fine.

670 1820 over '19. Nearly fine.

671 1820 Close date. Fine.

672 1820 Wide date. Very good.

673 1821 Close date. Fine.
674 1822 Head worn. Good.
675 1823 and 1824. Good. 2 pcs.
676 1825 Sharp; very fine.
677 1826 Nearly fine.
678 1827 Good.
679 1828 Fine.
680 1829 Sharp; very fine.
681 1830 Very good.
682 1831 Sharp; very fine.
683 1832 Sharp; very fine.
684 1833 Fine.
685 1834 Large date; rev., small lettering. Sharp; very fine.
686 1835 Very good.
687 1836 Old type; fine.
688 1836 Reeded edge. Very good; scarce.
689 1837 Fine, nicked.
690 1838 Very good.
691 1839 O under bust. Very fine; scarce.
692 1839 Liberty seated. Fine.
693 1840 *Orleans m.* Drapery under elbow. Fine.
694 1841 *Orleans m.* Very fine.
695 1842 Fine.
696 1843, 1844. *Orleans m.* Very good. 2 pcs.
697 1845 *Orleans m.* Sharp, very fine.
698 1846 *Orleans m.* Fine.
699 1847, 1848 *Orleans m.* Nearly fine. 2 pcs.
700 1849 Fine.
701 1850 *Orleans m.* Fine.
702 1851 *Orleans m.* Nearly fine.
703 1852 *Orleans m.* Fine; *rare.*
704 1853 Arrows, *Orleans m.* Very fine.
705 1854 *Orleans m.* Sharp, very fine.
706 1855 *Orleans m.* Sharp, very fine.
707 1856 *Orleans m.* Uncirculated.
708 1857 *Orleans m.* Very fine.
709 1858 *Orleans m.* Fine.

710 1859 *Orleans m.* Sharp, uncirculated.
711 1859 Large S for *San Fr.* Uncirculated, *rare.*
712 1859 Small S. Fine, scarce.
713 1860 *Orleans m.* Uncirculated; scarce.
714 1860 *San Francisco m.* Very fine, *rare.* Not in Davis collection.
715 1861 Uncirculated.
716 1861 *San Francisco m.* Sharp; uncirculated.

QUARTER DOLLARS.

717 1796 Well struck, the date, stars and legend almost fine, head somewhat worn. Very good; *rare.*
718 1804 Head worn, very good for date. *Rare.*
719 1805 Fine for date; scarce.
720 1805 Ordinary condition. 4 pcs.
721 1806 Hair worn. Very good.
722 1806, 1807 (2). Considerably circulated. 3 pcs.
723 1807 Good.
724 1815 Very good; scarce.
725 1818 Very good. 2 pcs.
726 1819 Sharp; fine.
727 1820 Very fair.
728 1821 Cracked die. Sharp; fine.
729 1822, 1824. Good, much circulated. 2 pcs.
730 1825 Sharp, uncirculated.
731 1828 Fine.
732 1831 Very fine.
733 1832 Fine.
734 1833, 1834, 1835 (2). Very good. 4 pcs.
735 1836 Perfect and cracked die. Very good. 2 pcs.
736 1837 Very fine.
737 1838 Bust of Liberty. Fine.
738 1838 Liberty seated. Very fine.
739 1839 Very fine.
740 1840 Drapery under elbow, *Orleans m.* Fine.
741 1841, 1842. *Orleans m.* Good. 2 pcs.
742 1843 Sharp, uncirculated.
743 1844 Fine.

744 1845 Fine.
745 1846 Fine.
746 1847, 1848. Fine. 2 pcs.
747 1849 Extremely fine.
748 1850 Uncirculated.
749 1851 Fine.
750 1852 Uncirculated.
751 1853 Without arrows at side of date. Fine, *rare.*
752 1853 Arrows, *Orleans m.* Sharp, uncirculated.
753 1854, 1856. Very good. 2 pcs.
754 1857 *Orleans m.* Uncirculated.
755 1858 *Orleans m.* Sharp, uncirculated.
756 1859 *Orleans m.* Fine.
757 1860 *Orleans m.* Very fine.
758 1861 Uncirculated.

DIMES.

759 1796 Break in die below lower left star; hair worn. Good, *rare.*
760 1797 13 stars. Hair worn. Very good, *rare.*
761 1798 over '97. Good, soldered in centre, *rare.*
762 1801 Good; *rare.*
763 1802 Fair, date plain; *rare.*
764 1804 Legend, date and stars to right plain; stars to left weak. Good, *rarest* of the Dimes.
765 1805 Fair and good. 2 pcs.
766 1807 Very fair.
767 1809 Good.
768 1811 Very good.
769 1814 Small date; very good.
770 1820 Large date. Very fine.
771 1821 Small date. Fine.
772 1822 Head worn from circulation, date and stars good; *rare.*
773 1823 over 22 Fine, scarce.
774 1824 over 22 Fair, pierced.
775 1825 Very good.
776 1827 Very fine.

777 1828 Large date; very good.
778 1828 Small date; very fine.
779 1829 Very fine.
780 1830 Polished planchet; uncirculated.
781 1831 Very fine.
782 1832 Very fine.
783 1833 Good.
784 1834 Uncirculated.
785 1835 Very fine.
786 1836 Uncirculated.
787 1837 Bust of Liberty. Very fine.
788 1837 Liberty seated. Very fine.
789 1837 Duplicates of both types. Good. 2 pcs.
790 1838 Liberty seated. *Orleans m.*; very good.
791 1838 Duplicate. Same condition.
792 1838 Liberty seated, stars. Polished planchet, sharp, uncirculated.
793 1838 Duplicate. Fine.
794 1839 Uncirculated.
795 1840 Without drapery under elbow. Very fine.
796 1841 Very fine.
797 1842 Uncirculated.
798 1843 Polished planchet; very fine.
799 1844, fair; 1845, *O.*, good. 2 pcs.
800 1846 Nearly fine; scarce.
801 1847, 1849, *O.* Good and very good. 2 pcs.
802 1848 Uncirculated.
803 1849 Uncirculated.
804 1850 Uncirculated.
805 1851 *Phil. and O. m.* Very good. 2 pcs.
806 1852 Very fine.
807 1853 Without arrows. Good.
808 1853 Arrows, *O.* Sharp, uncirculated.
809 1854 *O.* Fine.
810 1855 Very good.
811 1856 Large and small date. Good and fine. 2 pcs.
812 1857 *O.* Uncirculated.
813 1858 and 1859. Very fine. 2 pcs.

814 1860 Uncirculated.
815 1861 Brilliant impression; uncirculated.

HALF DIMES AND THREE CENTS.

816 1794 Damaged or plugged over forehead, and nicked in the field. Very good, *rare.*
817 1795 Good, nicked on reverse.
818 1795 Poor, pierced. 2 pcs.
819 1796 Pierced over head. Good.
820 1797 16 Stars. Nearly fine, *rare.*
821 1797 Duplicate. Scratched, good.
822 1800 Nicked in the hair. Very good.
823 1801 Fine; *rare.*
824 1803 Fair, date plain. *Rare.*
825 1805 Two cuts on edge. Good, *very rare.*
826 1829 Very fine.
827 1830, 1831. Good and fine. 2 pcs.
828 1832, 1833, 1834, 1835. Very fine. 4 pcs.
829 1835 Large and small date. Uncirculated. 2 pcs.
830 1836, 1837. Fine and good. 2 pcs.
831 1837 Bust of Liberty. Uncirculated.
832 1837 Liberty seated. Brilliant, sharp and uncirculated.
833 1838 Liberty seated, stars. Uncirculated.
834 1839 Sharp and uncirculated.
835 1840 Drapery below elbow. Brilliant, sharp, uncirculated.
836 1841, 1842, 1843. Very fine. 3 pcs.
837 1844 Fine, scarce.
838 1845 Very fine.
839 1846 Good; *rare.*
840 1847 Fine.
841 1848 Large date. Good.
842 1848 Small date. Brilliant, sharp, uncirculated.
843 1849 Uncirculated.
844 1850 *Phil. and O. m.* Very fine and good. 2 pcs.
845 1851 *Orleans m.* Very fine.
846 1852 Very fine.

847 1853 With and without arrows. Very fine. 2 pcs.

848 1854, 1855, *O.*, 1856. Fine. 3 pcs.

849 1857 *O.*, 1858, 1859, *O.*, 1860, 1861. Fine to uncirculated. 5 pcs.

850 THREE CENTS 1850. Liberty cap in rays; rev., III in wreath. Brilliant, uncirculated, scarce.

851 1851, 1852. Very fine. 2 pcs.

852 1853, 1854. Good. 2 pcs.

853 1855 Very good; scarce.

854 1856, 1857. Very good. 2 pcs.

855 1858 Uncirculated.

856 1859, 1860, 1861. Very fine and uncirculated. 3 pcs.

857 Duplicate of last number. Very fine. 3 pcs.

CENTS.

858 1793 Head of Liberty with flowing hair; rev., chain, UNITED STATES OF AMERI. Light impression, entire surface somewhat corroded; rev., fine. Very rare. Monograph U. S. Cents and Half Cents, No. 1.

859 1793 Head of Liberty without dot after legend and date; rev., chain, UNITED STATES OF AMERICA. Good, scarce. M. No. 3.

860 1793 Wreath Cent, leaves and bars on edge. Very good, scarce. M. No. 6.

860*a* 1793 Liberty cap. Poor, yet everything distinct. *Rare.*

861 1794 Head of Liberty. Similar to the Liberty cap of 1793. Good, but date very weak. Double chin variety; *rare.* M. No. 2, 1st rev.

862 1794. Fine impression, the 4 in date without horizontal stand, for which reason Dr. Maris called this variety "Standless four." M. No. 9.

863 1794 Young Head variety. Good, scarce. M. No. 4.

864 1794 Very fair. Varieties of "the Plicae." 3 pcs.

865 1795 Thin planchet; rev., ONE CENT in centre of wreath. Sharp, beautiful impression, the planchet slightly defective on right obverse edge. Uniform light bronze color; uncirculated. *Very rare.*

866 1795 Similar to last, but from different obv. and rev. dies, *edge milled*, a peculiarity I have observed in no other specimen. Very good, large nick on reverse.

867 1795 Different obv.; rev., ONE CENT high in wreath. Very good.

868 1796 Liberty cap. Wide date, a break in die follows upper line of letters in legend, another in the field from mouth to border. Brilliant, sharp impression of light olive color, unfortunately lightly nicked on cheek and hair, and parts of CENT and wreath blurred from defective planchet. *Very rare.*

869 1796 Draped bust. Sharp, uncirculated impression, with considerable original color, struck on a rough planchet. A beautiful and *very rare* Cent.

870 1796 Draped bust. From different obv. and rev. dies. Very good.

871 1797 Close date. Small break in die through cheek. Fine impression, olive color. Uncirculated.

872 1797 Wide date. Nearly fine.

873 1797 Fair and good. 3 pcs.

874 1798 Break in die on rev. Dark, fine.

875 1798 Same variety, good.

876 1799 Date very good, everything else poor; *rare.*

877 1800 With first 0 over 9. Very good.

878 1800 Perfect date. Obverse very fine; rev. good; planchet defective under date, still a desirable specimen.

879 1801 Very good.

880 1801 With $\frac{1}{000}$ on rev. Good.

881 1802 Fine; scarce.

882 1802 Very fair.

883 1803 Sharp, perfect impression, light olive, with traces of original red color; *rare.*

884 1804 Broken die. Nearly fine; *rare.*

885 1804 Broken die. Very fair for date; *rare.*

886 1805 Light brown, nicked on bust and in field, still nearly fine.

887 1806 Brown color. Very good; *rare.*

888 1807 over '06. Good.

889 1807 Perfect date and die. Fine; *rare.*

890 1807 Duplicate of last. Good. 2 pcs.

891 1808 Very good.

892 1808 Good.

893 1809 Good; very scarce.

894 1810 Fine impression; brown color, with black spots.
895 1811 over '10. Sharp, dark, very fine but slightly mis-struck.
896 1811 Perfect date. Very good.
897 1812 Sharp impression. Dark, extremely fine.
898 1813 Brown color, nicked in field. Fine, scarce.
899 1813 Good.
900 1814 The 4 in date with crosslet. Olive color, sharp, uncirculated.
901 1814 Duplicate. Dark brown, sharp and uncirculated.
902 1814 Another. Good.
903 1814 Plain 4. Light bronze, sharp, uncirculated.
904 1814 Duplicate of last. Very good.
905 1816 Connected milling from break in die. Sharp, uncirculated.
906 1817 Close date. Olive color; uncirculated.
907 1817 Fair.
908 1817 Ffteen stars. Fine, scarce.
909 1818 Stars to left rounded. Brilliant olive, uncirculated.
910 1818 Very fine.
911 1818 Good.
912 1819 Very fine.
913 1820 Fine.
914 1821 Very good; scarce.
915 1822 Fine.
916 1822 Good and very good. 2 pcs.
917 1823 over '22. Very good.
918 1824 Very good.
919 1825 Sharp, beautiful impression, of fine olive color. Uncirculated, nicked on cheek.
920 1826 Olive color, very fine.
921 1827 Fine, bulging in field from nick on reverse.
922 1828 Large date. Sharp, very fine.
923 1828 Same variety. Fair and very good. 2 pcs.
924 1828 Small date. Stars very slightly rounded. Sharp, uncirculated, a beautiful Cent.
925 1829 Brown color, fine.
926 1830 Brown color, nearly fine.

927 1830 Good and very good. 2 pcs.
928 1831 Olive color, very fine.
929 1832 Brown color, fine.
930 1833 Sharp, perfect impression. Dull red; uncir.
931 1833 Fine.
932 1834 Fine.
933 1835 Slightly nicked on edge and cheek. Fine.
934 1835 Good.
935 1836 Broken die. Extremely fine; slight nick on cheek.
936 1837 Stars not all sharp. Dull red; uncirculated.
937 1838 Dotted hair-string. Sharp; uncirculated.
938 1838 Duplicate. Stars not as sharp as last; uncir.
939 1839 '38 head. Very good.
940 1839 Booby head. Very fine.
941 1839 Booby head. Very good.
942 1839 '40 head. Fine.
943 1839 '40 head. Good.
944 1840 Small date. Very fine.
945 1841 Fine.
946 1842 Large date. Very fine.
947 1842 Small date. Nearly fine.
948 1843 Obv. and rev. of '42. Very fine.
949 1845 Brilliant, uncirculated; small spot, which can easily be removed.
950 1846 Dull red; sharp, uncirculated.
951 1846 Fine, nicked.
952 1847 Sharp and uncirculated.
953 1847 Very good.
954 1848 Sharp, uncirculated.
955 1849 Uncirculated.
956 1849 Uncirculated.
957 1850 Dull red; uncirculated.
958 1851 Uncirculated.
959 1851 Uncirculated. 2 pcs.
960 1851 Brown color; uncirculated. 2 pcs.
961 1852 Dull red; sharp, uncirculated.

962 1852 Same condition as the preceding.
963 1852 Very fine. 2 pcs.
964 1853 Dull red, a little spotted. Uncirculated.
965 1854 Dull red; uncirculated.
966 1854 Very fine. 2 pcs.
967 1855 Dark olive; uncirculated.
968 1855 Very fine and uncirculated. 2 pcs.
969 1855 Slanting 55. Dull red; uncirculated.
970 1856 Dull red; uncirculated.
971 1856 Uncirculated.
972 1856 Very fine. 2 pcs.
973 1857 Large date, olive color. Uncirculated.
974 1857 Large date. Very fine.
975 1857 Large date. Very fine.
976 1857 Large date. Very fine.
977 1857 Small date. Proof.
978 1857 Small date. Uncirculated.
979 1857 Small date. Very fine.
980 Cents. 1795–1856. Not consecutive; early dates poor.
982 1854 Pattern Cent. Head of Liberty without stars; rev., ONE CENT in wreath. Copper, very fine.
983 1854 Pattern Cent. Flying eagle and stars; rev., ONE CENT in wreath. Copper proof.
984 1855 Flying eagle Cent. Copper; fine.
985 1855 Same struck in nickel. Fine.
986 1856 Nickel Cent. Flying eagle; fine and scarce.
987 1857, '58, '59, '60, '61, '63, '64 Nickel Cents. Very fine to proof. 10 pcs.
988 1864 and 1865. Bronze 2 (1) and 1 Cents; 1883 Nickel V (2). Uncirculated. 6 pcs.

HALF CENTS.

989 1793 Fine and *rare*. Monograph No. 2.
990 1794 Very fair; scarce.
991 1795 Thick planchet, lettered edge. Good, scarce.
992 1795 Thin planchet, with break in die on rev. Obv. fine; rev. good, *rare*.

993 1797 Very good; scarce.
994 1797 Fair.
995 1800 Good; scarce.
996 1802 Very fair; *rare*.
997 1803, '04 (var.), '05, '06. Good. 8 pcs.
998 1806 With and without stems to wreath. Good and very good. 4 pcs.
999 1807 Good. 3 pcs.
1000 1808 Fine; scarce.
1001 1809 Very fine.
1002 1810 Good; scarce.
1003 1810 and 1811 (1). Fair. 3 pcs.
1004 1811 Very good; scarce.
1005 1825, '28 (12 and 13 stars), '29. Very good and fine. 5 pcs.
1006 1828 12 (1) and 13 stars. Fine. 5 pcs.
1007 1829, '32, '33, '34, '35. Very fine. 5 pcs.
1008 1837 Half Cent worth of pure copper. Fine.
1009 1849 Large date. Very good. 2 pcs.
1010 1850 Nearly proof obverse; scarce.
1011 1851, '53, '54. Fine. 3 pcs.
1012 1856 Nearly proof; scarce.
1013 1795–1854. Several dates missing. A few poor, others good to fine, one pierced. 28 pcs.
1014 Copperheads or War Tokens. Fine, select lot. 81 pcs.

COLONIAL COINS.

1015 Massachusetts. 1652. Oak tree Shilling. Large oval planchet; very good, *rare*.
1016 1652 Pine tree Shilling. Large planchet.
1017 1652 Pine Tree Shilling. Small planchet; fine.
1018 1652 Pine Tree Shilling. Small pl., rather poor.
1019 1652 Pine Tree Sixpence. Very good; misstruck.
1020 1652 Pine Tree Sixpence. Good, pierced.
1021 1652 Pine Tree Threepence. Good; *rare*.
1022 1652 Wyatt's Shil., 6, 3 and 2d. Very fine. 4 pcs.

1023 James II. Plantation $\frac{1}{24}$ Real. Tin; fine, scarce.

1024 Rosa Americana. 1722. Twopence. Bust of George I; rev., blooming rose. Very good; nicked in centre.

1025 1722 Penny. Type of preceding. Good.

1026 1722 Halfpenny. Good, nicked on edge.

1027 1722 Halfpenny. Same; rev., ROSA AMERI. Very fair, *rare*.

1028 1723 Twopence. Bust; rev., crowned rose. Very good; rev., fair.

1029 1723 Twopence and Penny. Very fair. 2 pcs.

1030 1722 Wood Halfpenny. Bust of George I; rev., Hibernia seated with harp at her right. Very good; *rare*.

1031 1723 Wood Halfpence. Usual type; die varieties. Fine. 2 pcs.

1032 1723 Halfpence. Good. 2 pcs.

1033 1723 Wood Farthing. Fine; *rare*.

1034 Colonies Françaises. 1721, 1767, with and without R. F. Fair and good. 4 pcs.

1035 1766 Pitt Token. Bust; rev., ship, AMERICA. Very fine.

1036 Virginia. 1773. Halfpenny. Fine.

1037 1783 Nova Constellatio, U. S. Very good. 2 pcs.

1038 1785 Nova Constellatio. *U. S.* Very good. 2 pcs.

1039 1787 Fugio Cents. "States United" and "United States." Good, fine, and bright red; the latter probably a restrike. 3 pcs.

1040 Massachusetts. 1787. Cent. Horned eagle variety. Sharp; uncirculated.

1041 1787 Half Cent. Fine impression; uncirculated.

1042 1787 Half Cent. Very fine, but weak in centre.

1043 1787 Half Cents. Very good, one counterstamped C. 2 pcs.

1044 1788 Cent. Sharp, extremely fine.

1045 1788 Cent. Die variety. Fine.

1046 1788 Cents. Die varieties. Very good. 2 pcs.

1047 1788 Half Cent. Uncirculated.

1048 Vermont. 1785. VERMONTS. RES. PUBLICA. Fine.

1049 1785 VERMONTIS RES. PUBLICA. Good.

1050 1786 VERMONTENSIUM. Nearly fine.

1051 1786 Same type. Good. 2 pcs.

1052 Connecticut. 1787. Head left. Several die varieties. Fair to very good. 7 pcs.

1053 New Jersey. 1787, 1788 (1). Several die varieties. Good and very good. Desirable lot. 11 pcs.

1054 New York. 1787. Liberty seated to right (1), and left. Very fair. 3 pcs.

1055 1795 Talbot, Allum & Lee. N. Y. Cent; same obv., muled with English Halfpenny. Fine and uncirculated. 2 pcs.

1056 Kentucky Cent. Thin planchet; fine.

1057 Rhode Island satirical piece against the Americans. Island with fleeing soldiers, man-of-war on one side, boats on the other; rev., flagship. Brass, fine. 20.

1058 1796 Castorland Token. Copper, *cuivre* on edge. Uncirculated. All French medals and tokens with metal stamped on edge are restrikes and can now be had at the French mint. 20.

1059 Massachusetts Cents (5), Half Cent, Vermont (2), New Jersey (3), etc. Poor to very fair. 2 pierced. 16 pcs.

PRESIDENTS OF THE UNITED STATES; ARMY AND NAVY.

Bronze, and in the finest condition; exceptions will be noted.

1060 Horatio Gates. 1777. Bust; rev., surrender of Burgoyne at Saratoga. 35.

1061 John Paul Jones. 1779. Bust; rev., engagement off Coast of Scotland. Impression from broken dies. 36.

1062 Daniel Morgan. 1781. Indian queen crowning victorious general; rev., view of action at Cowpens. 36.

1063 John E. Howard. 1781. For Cowpens. 29.

1064 Thomas Truxton. Bust; rev., naval engagement. Vote of Congress, 1800. 36.

1065 Thomas Jefferson. 1801. Bust; rev., hands clasped under a tomahawk and calumet, PEACE AND FRIENDSHIP. 48.

1066 James Madison. 1809. Bust; rev. as last. 40.

1067 Isaac Hull. 1812. Bust; rev., engagement between the Constitution and Guerriere. 41.

1068 Jacob Jones. 1812. Bust; rev., engagement between the Wasp and Frolic. 41.

1069 Stephen Decatur. 1812. Bust; rev., engagement between the United States and Macedonian. 41.

1070 William Bainbridge. 1812. Bust; rev., engagement between the Constitution and Java. 41.

1071 James Lawrence. 1813. Bust; rev., engagement between the Hornet and Peacock. 41.

1072 Col. George Croghan. 1813. Bust; rev., attack of stockade at Sandusky by Indians. 41.

1073 O. H. Perry. 1813. Bust; PRESENTED BY THE GOVERNMENT OF PENNSYLVANIA: rev., defeat and capture of the English fleet on Lake Erie, Sept. 10. 38.

1074 Same obv.; rev., TO ——— in wreath, FOR BRAVERY IN THE NAVAL ACTION ON LAKE ERIE, etc. 38.

1075 Edward R. McCall. 1813. Bust: rev., engagement between the Enterprise and Boxer. 41.

1076 W. Burrows. 1813. Mortuary trophy; rev., same as last. 41.

1077 Gen. William H. Harrison. 1813. Bust; rev., Columbia crowning a trophy inscribed FORT MEIGS, BATTLE OF THE THAMES. 41.

1078 Governor Isaac Shelby. 1813. Bust; rev., view of the battle of the Thames. 41.

1079 Louis Warrington. 1814. Bust; rev., engagement between the Peacock and Epervier. 41.

1080 Johnston Blakeley. 1814. Bust; rev., engagement between the Wasp and Reindeer. 41.

1081 Gen. Winfield Scott. 1814. Bust; rev., RESOLUTION OF CONGRESS; BATTLES OF CHIPPEWA JULY 5, NIAGARA JULY 25, etc., in wreath. 41.

1082 General Peter B. Porter. 1814. Bust; rev., Victory dictates to Fame the names of victories, Chippewa, Niagara, Erie, etc. 41.

1083 Gen. Jacob Brown. 1814. Bust; rev., trophy guarded by American eagle. For Chippewa, Niagara, and Erie. 41.

1084 Brig. Gen. James Miller. 1814. Bust; rev., view of the battle. For Chippewa, Niagara, and Erie. 41.

1085 Duplicate of last. Thin planchet, dull bronze. 41.

1086 Brig. Gen. Eleazer W. Ripley. 1814. Bust; rev. Fame hanging shield inscribed CHIPPEWA, NIAGARA, ERIE to palm tree. 41.

1087 Gen. Edmund P. Gaines. 1814. Bust; rev. Victory crowning a trophy, BATTLE OF ERIE. 41.

1088 Theodore Macdonough. 1814. Bust; rev., view of the naval engagement on Lake Champlain. 41.

1089 Stephen Casson. 1814. Bust; rev., same as last. 41.

1090 Gen. Alexander Macomb. 1814. Bust; rev., view of the battle at Plattsburgh, Sept. 11. 41.

1091 R. H. Eagle. Bust; rev., same as in 1088. 41.

1092 Gen. Andrew Jackson. 1815. Bust; rev., Victory dictating to Fame, who inscribes "Orleans" on scroll. For the battle of New Orleans, January 8. 41.

1093 Charles Stewart. 1815. Bust; rev., engagement between the Constitution and the Levant and Cyane. 41.

1094 James Biddle. 1815. Bust; rev., capture of the British ship Penguin by the Hornet, off Tristan d'Acunha. 41.

1095 James Monroe. 1817. Bust; rev., hands clasped, PEACE AND FRIENDSHIP. 40.

1096 John Quincy Adams. 1825. Bust; rev., same as last. 40.

1097 Andrew Jackson. 1829. Bust; rev., same. 40.

1098 Martin Van Buren. 1837. Bust; rev., same. 40.

1099 John Tyler. Bust; rev., APRIL IV MDCCCXLI in wreath. 40.

1100 James K. Polk. Bust; rev., MARCH MDCCCXLV in wreath. 40.

1101 James K. Polk. 1845. Bust; rev., hands clasped, PEACE AND FRIENDSHIP. 32.

1102 Rescue of crew of Brig Somers before Vera Cruz, Dec., 1846. 36.

1102*a* Duplicate of last. Equally fine. 36.

1103 Gen. Winfield Scott. Bust; rev., views of seven battles in Mexico, RESOLUTION OF CONGRESS MARCH 9, 1848. 56.

1104 Gen. Winfield Scott. Bust; rev., view of the battle of Buena Vista within circle formed of two serpents. RESOLUTION OF CONGRESS MAY 9 1848. 56.

1105 Gen. Winfield Scott. Small bust in trophy over inscribed tablet; rev., eagle on column. The Virginia medal for victories in Mexico. 56.

1106 General Zachary Taylor. Bust; rev., RESOLUTION OF CONGRESS JULY 16 1846, PALO ALTO MAY 8TH 1846, RESACA DE LA PALMA MAY 9 1846. 40.

1107 Gen. Zachary Taylor. Same obv.; rev., RESOLUTION OF CONGRESS MARCH 2D 1847 MONTEREY SEPTEMBER 1846 in wreath. 40.

1108 Gen. Zachary Taylor. 1849. Bust; rev., PEACE AND FRIENDSHIP. 49.

1109 Millard Fillmore. 1850. Bust; rev., farmer, Indian and U. S. flag. 49.

1110 Duplicate of last. Fine. 49.

1111 Franklin Pierce. 1853. Bust; rev., same as last. 49.

1112 James Buchanan. 1857. Bust; rev., Western scene, Indian scalping prisoner, on broad border. 49.

1113 James Buchanan. Similar bust; rev., IN COMMEMORATION OF THE FIRST EMBASSY FROM JAPAN TO THE UNITED STATES 1860. 49.

1114 James Buchanan. Same obv.; rev., allegorical group, TO DR. FREDERICK ROSE, ASSISTANT SURGEON, ROYAL NAVY G. B. FOR KINDNESS AND HUMANITY TO OFFICERS AND CREW OF THE U. S. STEAMER SUSQUEHANNA. Obv. slightly spotted. 49.

1115 Abraham Lincoln. 1862. Bust; rev., Western scene, Indians on border as in 1112. 40.

1116 American Sloop of war St. Louis and Austrian Brig of war Hussar, in Bay of Smyrna; TO COMMANDER DUNCAN N. INGRAHAM, etc., FOR JUDICIOUS CONDUCT, JULY 1853, etc. 64.

1117 Com. M. C. Perry. Bust; rev., PRESENTED BY MERCHANTS OF BOSTON FOR TREATY WITH JAPAN 1854. etc. 41.

1118 Life Saving Medal. American shield displayed; rev., rescue of drowning youth. 41.

1119 Coast Survey Medal. FOR GALLANTRY AND HUMANITY DEC., 1846. 22.

1120 Arms of Philadelphia; rev., inscription commemorative of Captains Creighton, Low and Stouffer for rescue of passengers from wreck of steamer San Francisco. 48.

1121 Robert M. Patterson, Director U. S. Mint, 1835–1851. Bust; rev., inscription in wreath. Fine. 40.

1122 Washington before Boston; Franklin, rev., ERIPUIT COELO; John Paul Jones, rev., ships; William Washington and John E. Howard for Cowpens. Fine bronze medal in old morocco case. 29 to 43. 5 pcs.

COINS AND MEDALS OF GEORGE WASHINGTON.

1123 1783 Cents. Military bust; Unity States; double-head. Very good. 5 pcs.

1124 Double-head Cent. Fine.

1125 1783 Washington and Independence; rev., United States. Sharp, uncirculated; London restrike.

1126 1791 Cent. Bust; rev., large heraldic eagle. Good.

1127 Military bust left; rev., harp, NORTH WALES. Very good. 17. 2 pcs.

1128 Bust right; rev., "Success to the United States." Copper and brass, fine and good. 12 and 16. 2 pcs.

1129 1783 Military bust; rev., ship, HALFPENNY. Very good. 20.

1130 1795 Bust right; rev., shield, LIBERTY AND SECURITY. Good. 18.

1131 Funereal Medal. Bust in wreath, HE IS IN GLORY, THE WORLD IN TEARS; rev., urn, etc. Tin; pierced, fine original. 19.

1132 1789 Military bust, GEORGE WASHINGTON, PRESIDENT; rev., eagle displayed. Copper proof. 20.

1133 1792 Washington Half Dollars. Copper, brass and w.m. Copies, nearly proof. 3 pcs.

1134 Naked bust facing right by *Paquet*; rev., CABINET OF MEDALS U. S. MINT, 1860. Silver, mint state. 38.

1135 Duplicate of last. Bronze; mint state. 38.

1136 Naked bust left, eagle above; rev., view of the Crystal Palace, N. Y., 1853. W.m., very fine. 32.

1137 Small bust right in depressed circle; rev., Washington's equestrian statue at Union Square, N. Y., 1861. Silver, mint state. 32.

1138 Duplicates of last. Bronze and w.m.; mint state. 2 pcs.

1139 Same obverse; rev., blank. W.m., mint state.

1140 Same obverse; rev., ground floor Masonic Temple, 1859. Bronze; mint state. 32.

1141 Duplicate of last; bronze, same condition.

1142 Naked bust right; rev., agricultural trophy. Fine silver medal of the Lancaster Co. Agricultural and Mechanical Society, name engraved on the reverse. 29.

1143 Duplicate of last, without name on rev. Copper, mint state. 29.

1144 Another; same metal and condition as last.

1145 Old bust right; rev., fasces, sword and wreath on altar. COMMISS. RESIGNED; PRESIDENCY RELINQ. 1797. Bronze; very fine. 29.

1146 Same design. Bronze, fine. 25.

1147 Naked bust right by *Lovett*, WASHINGTON TEMPERANCE SOCIETY; rev., the temperance declaration. Copper, mint state. 27.

1148 Same design. Copper, brass, and w.m., mint state. 3 pcs.

1149 Same obv.; rev., home scene, THE HOUSE OF TEMPERANCE. Copper, mint state. 27.

1150 Same design. Cop., brass, and w.m., same condition. 3 pcs.

1151 Duplicates of 1147 and 1149. Two of each; brass and w.m., very fine. 4 pcs.

1152 Large bust by *Du Vivier;* rev., SERIES NUMISMATICA. Bronze, mint state. 26.

1153 Short, naked bust to left; rev., PRESENTED BY THE METROPOLITAN MECHANICS INSTITUTE, on label, around blank shield for name. Bronze, very fine. 24.

1154 Bust left, N & G TAYLOR CO PHILADELPHIA, etc. Brass, fine. 26.

1155 Long bust facing; rev., A MAN HE WAS TO ALL HIS COUNTRY DEAR in wreath, radiant eye above. W.m., very fine. 24.

1156 Draped bust in wreath of roses; rev., view of Mount Vernon. WASHINGTON'S RESIDENCE. Copper proof. 22.

1157 Same. W.m. proof. 2 pcs.

1158 Same bust in plain wreath of oak; rev. blank. W.m. proof. 22.

1159 Bust facing, UNITY OF GOVERNMENT, etc.; rev., HE IS A FREEMAN WHOM THE TRUTH MAKES FREE. Thick planchet, copper proof. 22.

1160 Washington on horseback. Brass calendars. Very fine. 22. 2 pcs.

1161 Small bust in oval; rev., CIVIC PROCESSION FEB 22D 1832. Copper and w.m., mint state. 21. 2 pcs.

1162 Bust right, GEORĠE WASHINGTON; rev., PRO PATRIA, BORN, etc., Baltimore monument, Edward Cogan's card. No dupl., cop. (3), and w.m., mint state. 20. 5 pcs.

1163 Duplicates. Cop. (1), and w.m., same condition. 3 pcs.

1164 Bust r., SECURITY; rev., Washington before Boston, Coin Safe. Cop. and brass, mint state. 21. 2 pcs.

1165 Bust r., BORN FEBRUARY 22 1732; obv., Washington's tomb, bust of Everett. Cop. and w.m., mint state. 20. 2 pcs.

1166 Naked bust r. by *Paquet;* rev., U. S. MINT OATH OF ALLEGIANCE, 1861. Thick planchet, silver, very fine. 20.

1167 Duplicate. Thick planchet, silver, very fine. 20.

1168 Another. Bronze, very fine. 20.

1169 Long military bust to left, CINCINNATUS OF AMERICA; rev., "The Union must and shall be preserved," "Industry produces wealth," John K. Curtis's card. Copper (3), brass (1) and w.m. Mint state. 20. 7 pcs.

1170 Short bust within branches of palm and laurel; rev., Washington on horseback to right, GEN. GEORGE WASHINGTON 1776. Silver, mint state. 20.

1171 Washington on horseback, as in last number; rev., bust, WASHINGTON in tressure of stars, headquarters at Valley Forge, Tappan, Newburgh, the home of W. at Mount Vernon. Copper, mint state, no duplicate. 20. 6 pcs.

1172 Duplicates of last. Brass, mint state. 6 pcs.

1173 Same obv., rev., Mount Vernon, Valley Forge, Tappan and Newburgh. Copper, mint state. 20. 4 pcs.

1174 Same as last. Brass, very fine. 4 pcs.

1175 Another set, as 1171. W.m. proof. 6 pcs.

1176 Duplicates as 1173. W.m. proof. 6 pcs.

1177 Washington on horseback to left; rev., "Siege of Boston 1775–6," headq. at Valley Forge, Mount Vernon, R. Lovett's card. Copper (4), brass (2) and w.m. Mint state. 20. 9 pcs.

1178 Same obv. as 1170; rev., WASHINGTON in radiant tressure of stars. Silver, mint state. 20.

1179 Same as last. Nickel, copper, brass and w.m. Mint state. 20. 6 pcs.

1180 Short bust; rev., TIME INCREASES HIS FAME. Bronze, thick pl., mint state. 18.

1181 Washington on horseback to right, GEORGE WASHINGTON above; rev., BORN FEB 22 1732, etc. in circle of stars and Liberty caps. Copper, brass and w.m. Mint state. 18. 3 pcs.

1182 Small military bust in sunken circle, 13 stars in tressures on border; rev., Washington's headquarters, No. 1 to 10 complete. Copper proof. 18. 10 pcs.

1183 Another set. Copper, dull proofs. 18. 10 pcs.

1184 Another set. Brass proof. 18. 10 pcs.

1185 Same obv.; rev., W. on horseback, mortuary inscription, bust of Franklin. Copper, dull proofs. 18. 3 pcs.

1186 Same as last. Brass (2) and w.m. proof. 3 pcs.

1187 Same bust, but border of 32 small pointed arches; rev., headquarters No. 1, 2 (3), bust of Franklin. Copper (3) and brass, fine to proof. 18. 5 pcs.

1188 Same obv. as last, with addition of 32 small stars on border; rev., headquarters, lacking No. 4. W.m. proof. 18. 9 pcs.

1189 Bust of Wash. as in 1182; rev., bust and border with stars as in last No. Copper, dull proof. 18.

1190 Another. Copper proof.

1191 Duplicate of 1189; also obv. as 1188, rev., headquarters No. 1, mortuary inscription. Copper (1) and w.m. proof. 18. 3 pcs.

1192 Bust l.; rev., Ridgeway and Shelby Agr. Soc. 1858. W.m. proof. 18.

1193 Undraped bust l., without inscription; rev., Liberty cap and circle of rays, arms of Washington, statues at Richmond and New York, U. S. shield with date of birth and death, tomb. Copper proof. 18. 6 pcs.

1194 Draped bust, GEORGE WASHINGTON; rev., arms as last and combinations of revs. Copper proof, no duplicates. 18. 14 pcs.

1195 Bust in arch, PATRIAE PATER 1732; rev., E. Hill, F. C. Key, Key, Coin and Medal collectors. Copper (1), brass (1) and w.m., very fine and proof. 18. 7 pcs.

1196 Same without arch; rev., "Providence left him childless," "Virtue, Liberty and Independence." Copper (1), brass (2) and w.m., very fine and proof. 18. 5 pcs.

1197 Short bust r., in broad wreath of laurel, WASHINGTON above: rev., "The hero of American Independence," Jos. H. Merriam's card. Copper (2) and w.m. proof. 17. 4 pcs.

1198 Bust r., rev., arms of New York. W.m., fine, pierced. 17.

1199 Spiel-marks and Jetons. Brass, fine to proof, all with bust of Washington. 13 to 20. 18 pcs.

1200 E. Ivins, T. Brimelow, Temperance Tokens and store cards, all with bust of Washington. Copper and brass, fine to proof. 14 and 15. 8 pcs.

1201 Small bust r., PATER PATRIAE above; rev., A MEMORIAL OF THE WASHINGTON CABINET MAY 1859 in wreath. Silver, bronze and copper, mint state. 14. 3 pcs.

1202 Draped bust left, PATER PATRIAE at sides; rev., undraped bust of Washington, name above, dates of birth and death on border. Copper (2), and brass, fine, thick. 14. 4 pcs.

1203 Same obv.; rev., A. B. Sage's Card and Numismatic Raffle. Copper (2), brass and w.m., very fine. 14. 4 pcs.

1204 Undraped bust as on rev. of 1202; rev., monument at Baltimore. Silver, cop., nickel, br., and w.m. proof. 14. 5 pcs.

1205 Duplicates. Cop., br., and w.m. proof. 3 pcs.

1206 Bust; rev., Martha W.; another bust, rev. trophy; another with Wm. Leggett Bramhall's card, etc. Bronze, nickel, cop., and w.m., very fine. 12 to 14. 8 pcs.

1207 Draped bust l.; rev., tomb. Silver proof. 13.

1208 Bust of Wash., rev., bust of Lincoln; same bust, rev., BORN 1732 DIED 1799. Silver proof. 12. 2 pcs.

1209 Duplicates of last; another, smaller bust, rev., bust of Jackson. Silver, very fine and proof. 12. 3 pcs.

1210 Draped bust over crossed branches of palm; rev., A. B. Sage's Card. Wm., fine. 10.

1211 Copperheads or War Tokens. All with bust of Washington. Silver (1), cop., brass, and w.m. (1). Uncirculated. 24 pcs.

POLITICAL MEDALS, ETC.

1212 Bust of Washington surrounded by busts of other Presidents down to Martin Van Buren; rev., names in wreath. W.m., very fine. 30.

1213 James Madison. Bust r.; rev. eagle grasping agricultural implements and wreath, within which PROTECTION AGAINST INVASION IS DUE, FROM EVERY SOCIETY, TO THE PARTS COMPOSING IT. W.m. silvered, fine. 41.

1214 Andrew Jackson. Bust right, OLD HICKORY, etc.; rev., long biographical and mortuary inscription. Cop., br., and w.m., very fine. 22. 3 pcs.

1215 Jackson on horseback to left; rev., THE UNION MUST AND SHALL BE PRESERVED. Silver, very fine. 18.

1216 Duplicate of last; bust, rev., "We commemorate," etc.; bust, rev. funeral urn. Bronze, copper, and pewter (pierced). Good to very fine. 17 and 18. 3 pcs.

1217 Wm. H. Harrison. Bust left over semi-circle of stars; rev., Bunker Hill monument, HARRISON JUBILEE, 1840. Red bronze, mint state. 28.

1218 Same. Old bust right, TO THE HERO OF TIPPECANOE; rev., Bunker Hill monument. Copper and nickel, mint state. 26. 2 pcs.

1219 Same. Military bust l.; rev., log cabin, the PEOPLE'S CHOICE. Copper, mint state. 22.

1220 Same. Bust; rev., log cabins, "Go it Tip." Brass, all different, good, pierced. 15 to 18. 4 pcs.

1221 Henry Clay. Large draped bust; rev., recording angel inscribing his name, etc. on a monument. W.m., fine. 26.

1222 Same. Bust in wreath, name above; rev., Bunker Hill monument. Copper, brass and w.m. Very fine. 25. 3 pcs.

1223 Same obv.; rev., "Nominated by the Baltimore convention," etc. Nickel, Copper, brass and w.m. Very fine. 25. 4 pcs.

1224 Same. All different. Copper (2) and w.m. Good to fine, 2 pierced. 15 to 24. 6 pcs.

1225 Zachary Taylor. Military bust, NEVER SURRENDER; rev., tablet inscribed with names of victories in trophy. Bronze, mint state. 26.

1226 Taylor, Polk, Wm. H. Seward, Scott, Fillmore, Pierce, Buchanan, Fremont, Douglas, Bell, etc. Copper, brass and w.m., average fine, 7 pierced. 12 to 26. 24 pcs.

1227 Daniel Webster. Bust by *Wright*; rev., column surmounted by globe, LIBERTY AND UNION, etc. Bronze, fine. 48.

1228 Bust right, "Daniel Webster;" rev., "I still live" in wreath. Copper, very fine. 20.

1229 Martin Van Buren. Old bust l.; rev., biographical and mortuary inscription. Copper, brass and w.m. proof. 22. 3 pcs.

1230 Millard Fillmore. Bust r.; rev., "Be vigilant," etc., in wreath. Bronze, mint state. 22.

1231 Franklin Pierce. Military bust; rev., shield in trophy of flags, "United we stand," etc. W.m., fine. 26.

1232 James Buchanan. Bust; rev., eagle in radiant circle inscribed with names of States. Yellow brass, fine. 39.

1233 John C. Fremont. Bust; rev., inscription beginning "Born Jan: 21, 1813" and ending with "Defeated Stonewall Jackson 1862." Copper, brass and w.m. proof. 26. 3 pcs.

1234 Bust; rev., soldiers gathered around U. S. flag, "Fremont and Cochrane." W.m., fine. 22.

1235 Bust, "John C. Fremont for President 1860;" rev., military trophy. Nickel and brass, mint state. 20. 2 pcs.

1236 Duplicates of last. Same condition. 2 pcs.

1237 Stephen A. Douglas. Bust; rev., "Democratic candidate," etc. Copper and w.m., very fine. 26. 2 pcs.

1238 Ferrotypes. Fremont, Douglas, Breckenridge, Bell, Johnson, etc. 18 pcs.

1239 Abraham Lincoln 1860. Bust l.; rev., fowls on rail fence, "The great rail splitter," etc. Copper, mint state. 23.

1240 Bust r., "Abraham Lincoln for President 1864." Nickel and brass, very fine. 20. 2 pcs.

1241 Duplicates of last. Same condition. 2 pcs.

1242 Bust r., "Abraham Lincoln, in God we trust," 25c. under bust; rev., eagle, "United States of America," etc., 1864. Nickel, silvered, good, *rare*. 16.

1243 Abraham Lincoln. Medals, all with bust and no duplicates except three struck in different metals. Rare lot. Copper, brass and w.m. Average very fine. 8 pierced. 12 to 26. 28 pcs.

1244 Abraham Lincoln. Ferrotypes. 12 pcs.

1245 Busts of Bell, Douglas, Breckenridge; rev., "President's house." Copper, very fine. 14. 3 pcs.

1246 No submission to the North; rev., shield, President's house, the wealth of the South. Copper and brass, fine and uncirculated. 14. 4 pcs.

1247 No submission to the North (4); duplicates of 1245. Brass and nickel. Fine, 4 pierced. 14. 7 pcs.

1248 Winfield Scott. Bust to left; rev., shield and inscription commemorative of the great mass meeting at Union Square, N. Y., April 19, 1861. W.m., fine. 40.

1249 George B. McClellan. Bust within deep border of cannons by *Bridgens*; rev., eagle on a cannon, within wreath of laurel and oak, "He carries with him the prestige of success." A fine and rare medal, w.m. 51.

1250 Geo. B. McClellan. Medals; all different and very fine. Nickel, copper, brass and w.m. 3 pierced. 12 to 24. 12 pcs.

1251 Duplicates of last, copperheads or war tokens with McClellan's bust. Silver (1), copper, brass and w.m., fine, 2 pierced. 8 pcs.

1252 Geo. B. McClellan. Oval shell with bust; ferrotypes. 11 pcs.

1253 U. S. Grant (3), Sherman (2). Different, copper, brass and w.m., good to proof, 3 pierced. 18 to 20. 5 pcs.

1254 Loyal National League. Flags crossed and inscriptions. Silver, pierced, very fine. 23.

1255 Bombardment of Fort Sumter, Monitor and Merrimac, I am ready, Mass. for justice (2), Fireman's medal, Death to Traitors, etc. Brass and w.m., fine, one pierced. 12 to 22. 10 pcs.

1256 Arms of N. Y.; rev., N. Y. S. Vols. W. m., pierced, fine. 26.

1257 Bust of yeoman in star-spangled blouse; different revs. Copper and brass, very fine. 20. 2 pcs.

1258 Bombardment of Fort Sumter, battle between Monitor and Merrimac, Fireman's medal. Copper, brass, w.m.; very fine. 20 to 22. 3 pcs.

1259 Gallery of American Traitors; Floyd, Bell, Jeff Davis, etc. W.m., fine. 20.

1260 Bust of Gen. Anthony Wayne. Robinson's Historical Series No. 1. Copper proof. 22.

1261 Declaration of Independence; rev., "Jefferson was its honored author," etc. Silver, copper, nickel, brass and w. m. Very fine. 13. 5 pcs.

1262 Henry White's Calendar; Henry Cook's card, with "No surrender," etc. Brass and w.m., very fine. 25 and 27. 2 pcs.

1263 War Medal. Liberty seated, "Liberty and Union," etc.; rev., hands clasped, "Mayre Heights," Fredericksburg, Va., "May 3d 1863. 23d reg. P. V." W.m., with ribbon and bronze pins. Very good, *rare*. 31. In case.

JACKSONIAN TOKENS, STORE CARDS, ETC.

1264 Collection of Jacksonian or Hard Times Tokens. All different, several very fine and rare, average condition fine. Would cost $25 to duplicate from dealer's list. 32 pcs.

1265 Duplicates; also early store cards, size of the old copper cent. Average nearly fine; desirable lot for private collector or dealer. 55 pcs.

1266 Feuchtwanger Currency. 1837. Three Cents, with arms of New York. Fine, scarce.

1267 1837 Feuchtwanger Cents. Good to uncir. 5 pcs.

1268 Chicago, Ill. Baker & Moody; C. N. Holden & Co.; Pearson & Dana. Cop. and brass, fine. 18. 5 pcs.

1269 State of Indiana, 1855, No repeal; John Plane & Co., Belvidere, Ill. Copper, fine, first named pierced. 18. 2 pcs.

1270 Kentucky. Brown, Curtis & Vance, Sandford Duncan, H. Miller & Co., Louisville; S. T. Suit, Salt River Bourbon, 1850 (3). Cop., br., and w.m. (1). Very good and fine, one pierced. 18 to 22. 6 pcs.

1271 Michigan. Daniel Ball & Co.; J. Dimmick; Foster & Parry, Grand Rapids. Copper and brass, fine. 18. 6 pcs.

1272 Mississippi. Benj. F. Fotterall, Vicksburg. Copper and brass, very fine. 18. 2 pcs.

1273 State of Missouri. Nickel Half Dime. Very fair, scarce.

1274 E. Long, D. Nicholson, St. Louis. Copper and brass, very good to uncirculated. 18. 3 pcs.

1275 E. Jaccard & Co., St. Louis, with oval in shield for counterstamp. Very fine set, copper, brass and w.m. 18. 3 pcs.

1276 Eagle and shield, "St. Louis Post Office" above; rev., *State Savings Ass* (engraved). Copper, fine and *rare.* 18.

1277 Shield in trophy of flags, surmounted by eagle, "St. Louis post office"; rev., blank. Tin, fine and *rare.* 16.

1278 M. A. Abrahams, Weston, Mo. Bust; rev., "The people's outfitting store," etc. Yellow copper, fine and *rare.* 18.

1279 New Jersey. S. A. Whitney, Glassboro'. Brass, good. 17.

1280 New Orleans. N. C. Folger & Son. N. C. Folger; E. Jacobs; L. W. Lyons & Co.; Robt. Pilkin. Copper and brass, fine. 16 to 18. 7 pcs.

1281 Duplicates of last. Good to uncir. 4 pcs.

1282 Walton, Walter & Co., New Orleans, 1836; rev., "Fine cutlery, guns, pistols," etc. Brass, fine and *rare.* 21.

1283 New York. Chesebrough, Stearns & Co.; Doremus & Nixon (var); Fountain Blacking; Loder & Co. (var.). Cop. and br., one good, others uncirculated. 18. 9 pcs.

1284 Jennings, Wheeler & Co. All different, two with map of North America. Brass and w.m., uncirculated. 18. 4 pcs.

1285 E. Lyons. Magnetic powder and pills, etc. Brass, all different and very good, one pierced. 14 and 18. 4 pcs.

1286 Malcolm & Gaul; Metr. Ins. Co.; Root & Co.; Scovill Manf. Co.; Smith's Clocks; Lewis L. Squires & Sons; H. B. West's trained dogs. Cop. and brass, very fine. 18. 9 pcs.

1287 Wood's Minstrels. Quarter Dollar size; silver, fine.

1288 Patterson Bros., Buffalo; Wm. R. Brown, Saratoga; T. L. Kingsley & Son, Utica; duplicates of preceding nos. Cop. and br., two pierced, fair to fine. 8 pcs.

1289 A. C. Yates, Syracuse, N. Y. Copper and br., uncirculated. 18. 2 pcs.

1290 Ohio. Dodd, S. C. Erwin, Cincinnati. Copper and brass; very fine. 14 and 18. 5 pcs.

1291 John Shillito & Co., Cincinnati. Encased three cent postage stamp. Very good; *rare.*

1292 Pennsylvania. W. A. Drown & Co.; Saml. Hart & Co., (var.); James Harmstead; M. A. Root; W. H. Richardson; Sharpless Brothers; Smith, Murphy & Co., all Philadelphia. Copper and brass, one fair, balance very fine. 14 to 18. 10 pcs.

1293 Head of Liberty with coronet inscribed "Parasol;" in exergue "Philada;" rev., eagle. Copper, very fine. 18.

1294 William W. Long, Phila. Masonic card. Fine. 18.

1295 Peale's Museum. Bust; rev., "Admit the bearer," another with "15" engraved, instead of legend in wreath. Fine. 20. 2 pcs.

1296 Tennessee. Francisco & Co., "Nashville and Memphis." Copper and brass, very fine. 18. 2 pcs.

1297 Wisconsin. J. A. Hopkins, Milwaukee; A. B. Van Cott, Racine. Different, copper, very good. 18. 4 pcs.

1298 Virginia. James E. Wolff, Petersburg. Brass, fine. 16.

1299 W. B. Chapman, etc.; J. B. Wilson; J. Conrad; Dime and Half Dime bread tokens. Good to fine, nickel, brass, etc. 11 and 12. 6 pcs.

1300 James Ware. Drayman and cart; rev., 25 cents. Brass, fine. 18.

1301 Eagle; rev., "H. Wind good for 5 cents." Yellow copper, milled edge, thick, fine. 12.

1302 Copperheads or War Tokens. Very fine, mostly of the larger size. 20 pcs.

1303 Third Reformed Pres. Cong., N. Y. Communicant's token. Oval, w.m. proof. 19.

1304 Store Cards, etc. Includes C. Simmonds & Co., St. Thomas, No. Am. token, Morse's Literary depot, etc. Copper, brass and w.m., poor to fine, 4 pierced. 10 to 20. 17 pcs.

1305 Rubber Store Cards. Oval and round. 9 pcs.

1306 American Jetons and Spiel-marks. Large and small, fine. 10 pcs.

1307 Bust of Anthony Wayne; rev., inscription, Robinson's Hist. series, No. 1. Brass and w.m., nearly proof. 22. 2 pcs.

1308 Bust of Robert Fulton; rev., primitive steamboat. Same series No. 2. Copper, brass and w.m., nearly proof. 22. 3 pcs.

1309 A. B. Sage's Numismatic Gallery. Portraits of Bushnell, Bogert, Colburn, Dr. Lewis, Jandon, Chesley, Rust, Dodge. Copper, all different, nearly proof. 20. 9 pcs.

1310 A. B. Sage's Historical tokens. Nos. 1 to 14 inclusive. Copper, uncirculated or nearly proof; a rare set. 19. 14 pcs.

1311 Duplicates of last, Nos. 1, 7, 8, 9, 10, 11; same, Odds and Ends No. 1, 2, 3; same, Masonic medalets, No. 1; same, view of City Hall, N. Y.; rev., card. Copper, uncirculated or nearly proof. 19. 11 pcs.

1312 Odd Fellows' Hall, N. Y., 1847; rev., emblems. Tin, pierced, fine. 24.

1313 Brass Almanac. Eagle grasping shield; Illinois, 1855. 24.

1314 Great Air Ship, City of N. Y. Copper and w.m., nearly proof. 22. 2 pcs.

1315 John C. Heenan, Thos. Sayers, pugilists. Varieties, copper, and w.m., very fine. 20 to 22. 4 pcs.

1316 George Washington. Bust r.; rev., view of Mount Vernon. Silver, nearly proof. 22.

1317 Same. Bust right; rev., "A memorial," etc. Bronze, fine. 14. 3 pcs.

1318 Washington Half Dollar, Wm. Idler's card. Copper, brass and w.m., nearly proof. 22. 4 pcs.

1319 Baltimore. Monument; rev., "Pro patria." Silver, fine. 20.

1320 Fireman's Medal. 1860. Silver, fine. 20.

1321 B. Franklin, Edwin Forrest, Edward Everett. Bust, various revs. Silvered, copper, brass, tin, fine. 18 to 20. 5 pcs.

1322 Daniel Webster, Edwin Forrest. Bust, various revs. W.m., very fine. 18. 10 pcs.

1323 Stephen Girard. Statue; different revs. Copper and w.m., very fine. 20. 3 pcs.

1324 Bust of John Brown; rev., gibbet, 1859. W.m., proof. 20.

1325 Charles Stubenrauch, medallist, St. Louis, Mo.; rev., a coin press. Copper, very fine. 18.

1326 Bust to left in wreath; rev., "Leopold de Meyer's concert." Brass, fine. 18.

1327 Great Eastern, 1859. Two varieties, with three revs. Copper, brass and w.m., very fine. 20. 7 pcs.

1328 Constitution and Guerriere. 1812. Copper, brass and w.m., very fine. 20. 3 pcs.

1329 Atlantic Telegraph. 1858, two revs. Brass and w.m., fine. 20. 3 pcs.

1330 The Antiquary, Cupid on dolphin, with revs. of Curtis and Lovett's cards. Copper and w.m. proof. 20. 4 pcs.

1331 Bombardment of Fort Sumter; rev., inscr. Copper, nearly proof. 22.

1332 Witch on broomstick; rev., "Dedicated to coin and medal collectors." Silvered, copper, br. and w.m., very fine. 17. 5 pcs.

1333 Penn's Treaty. Cop., br. and w.m., v. fine. 20. 3 pcs.

1334 Deer, as on Higley copper; rev., Alfred Robinson's card. Nickel, cop., brass and w.m. proof. 18. 4 pcs.

1335 Mobile Jockey Club, two revs. Nickel, copper, brass and w.m., very fine. 18. 5 pcs.

1336 Delta Psi Fraternity, 1860. Brass and w.m., fine. 18. 2 pcs.

1337 U. S. Mint, First Steam Coinage, 1836. Bronze, thick and thin planchet, fine. 18. 2 pcs.

1338 Indian bust, 1860: rev., Flora Temple, F. B. Smith & Hartmann's card. Brass and w.m., fine. 18. 2 pcs.

1339 M. L. Marshall, Oswego, N. Y., 1860. Fisherman; rev., inscription. Silver proof. 18.

1340 Springfield Arsenal, Louis Kossuth, bust, rev., "Now, in the name of eternal truth," etc. Brass, fine, latter pierced. 18. 2 pcs.

1341 1778 "Non dependens status." Copper, copy, uncir.

1342 Store Cards, Medalets, etc. Cop. (1), br. (1), and w.m. Average fine, four pierced. 18 to 27. 10 pcs.

MISCELLANEOUS AMERICAN MEDALS.

1343 Bust of George II; rev., Colonist and Indian at council fire, "Let us look to the Most High," etc. Bronze, broken die, mint state. 28.

1344 Lafayette. Bust right; rev., "The defender," etc. Bronze, mint state. 28.

1345 Duplicate of last; nearly as fine.

1346 Th. Jefferson. Bust; rev., "Peace and friendship." Tin, good, probably cast. 35.

1347 James Buchanan. Bust, nearly facing; rev., radiant eagle, names of States between rays. W.m., very fine. 38. In case.

1348 John Pintard. Bust r.; rev., building of the N. Y. Historical Society. Bronze, mint state. 41. In case.

1349 Gallery to right; rev., wreath. The Peabody medal. Bronze, mint state. 26.

1350 Elisha Kent Kane. Bust over view of Arctic scenery; rev., ground floor of Masonic Temple. Bronze, very fine. 32.

1351 Same. Bust r.; "Dr. E. K. Kane;" rev., "Born 1822, died 1857," etc. Bronze, very fine. 24.

1352 Dr. Valentine Mott. Bust r.; rev., "University of New York, medical department," etc. W.m., very fine. 22.

1353 Dr. David Hosack. Bust right; rev., "Arts and science." Bronze, fine. 21.

1354 Philadelphia Exposition. 1876. The Commission medals, large (36) gilt and bronze; smaller (24) silver and gilt. Very fine or proof, in velvet lined morocco case. 4 pcs.

1355 Same. Commission medal. W.m. in morocco case. Proof. 36.

1356 1876 V. Christesen's Centennial medal, with bust of Washington and inscription "Let us have peace." W.m., proof. 33.

1357 1776 Continental Currency. Copies, issued in 1876. Copper and w.m. proof. 24. 2 pcs.

1358 1876 Figures at sides of Am. shield; rev., "Dedicated to the people of the United States," etc. W.m. proof. 27.

1359 1876 Memorial Hall; rev., struck within the International Exhibition. Copper gilt, proof. 16.

1360 Erie Canal. 1825. River-gods; rev., eagle over view of completed canal. Tin, very fine and scarce. 51.

1361 New York World's Fair, 1853. Globe, with allegorical representations of the four quarters of the earth; rev., view of the Crystal Palace. Tin, fine and rare medal. 47.

1362 Columbia seated, 1853; rev., view of N. Y. Crystal Palace. Bronze, very fine. 26.

1363 Duplicates of last. Bronze, tin; very fine. 2 pcs.

1364 American Institute, New York. Female figure, seated; rev., wreath. Copper, very fine. 18.

1365 College St. Francis Xavier, New York. Prize medal. Bronze, fine. 22.

1366 New Haven Bi-centennial. 1833. Settlers at Quinnipiack, 1633; rev., view of the city of New Haven, 1833. Bronze, fine. 35.

1367 St. Louis Agricultural and Mechanical Association. Set of 3 designs, size 24, silver; 28, gilt; 44, silver (?). Mint state. In morocco case. 3 pcs.

1368 Duplicates. Bronze and w.m., fine. 24 and 28. 2 pcs.

1369 Maine Agricultural Society. Award medal. Bronze, very fine. 28.

1370 Mississippi Agricultural Bureau. Eagle; rev., inscription in wreath. W.m., very fine. 28.

1371 New Jersey and New York State Agr. Societies; Nassau Waterworks. W.m., fine, last named pierced. 20 and 22. 3 pcs.

1372 Pa. Female College, Reward of Superior Merit, Temperance, Schiller, etc. Copper (1), and w.m., very fine, one pierced. 24 to 29. 6 pcs.

1373 SILK AND PAPER BADGES. Washington Monument, 1848, eight later, duplicates. 16 pcs.

1374 COLONIAL CURRENCY. Delaware, Maryland, New Jersey, Pennsylvania, Rhode Island, Virginia. One poor, balance good and fine. 17 notes.

1375 Massachusetts. 1782, Dec. 1. Five Shillings and sixpence, pine-tree note. Uncanceled; fine and *rare*.

1376 UNITED COLONIES. Philadelphia, 1775, May 10, $5; 1776, Feb. 17, $1, ½, 4; May 9, $2, 3, 5; Nov. 2d, $8. Two poor, balance very good. 8 notes.

1377 Baltimore, 1777, Feb. 26, $30; Yorktown, 1778, April 11, $6, 20. Very good and fine, scarce. 3 notes.

1378 Philadelphia. 1778, Sept. 26, $7 (2), 8, 30, 40, 50, 60; 1779, Jan. 14, $1, 45, 50. Fine. 10 pcs.

1379 POSTAGE CURRENCY. 5, 10, 25, 50 Cents. Cut edges, *A. B. Co.*, crisp, new. 4 notes.

1380 5 Cents, duplicates. New. 4 notes.

1381 FRACTIONAL CURRENCY. 5, 10, 25, 50 Cents. Bust of Washington in gold oval. Crisp, new. 4 notes.

1382 3 Cents. Bust of Washington. Crisp, new.

1383 10 Cents. Bust of Washington, gold numbers at corners, green back. Crisp, new.

1384 10 Cents. Same design, red back. Crisp, new, *rare*.

1385 5 Cents. Head of Clark. Good.

1386 25 Cents. Bust of Fessenden. Very fine.

1387 25 Cents. Same, but thick parchment paper, solid gold numbers at sides, gold numbers at back. Has been folded and somewhat circulated; *very rare*.

1388 50 Cents. Liberty seated and bust in centre, green backs. Crisp, new. 2 notes.

1389 50 Cents. Liberty seated, red back and gold numbers. Autographic signatures of Colby and Spinner. small cut on edge, thick parchment paper, somewhat circulated, *rare*.

1390 State Banks, etc. 5 cents to $10. Poor lot. 24 notes.

FOREIGN COINS AND MEDALS; SILVER.

1391 AUGSBURG. 1632. Large pine cone formed of 12 shields and Hebrew word, on ornate column, "Post nvbila phoebvs," monogram at each side; rev., four crowned shields in chain of fortifications, crowned shield between crowned monograms above. Very fine and *rare*. 48.

1392 AUSTRIA. Leopold. 1623. Crown. Cloaked bust right; rev., large crowned shield. Fine.

1393 Francis II. 1796. Crown. Very fair.

1394 1813 Busts jugata of Francis I, Alexander I and Frederic William; rev., inscription commemorative of the coalition against Napoleon I. Very fine. 30.

1395 BAVARIA. Maximilian Joseph. 1758. Crown. Fair.

1396 Ludwig I. 1827. Medallic Thaler for the customs-union with Wurtemberg. Very good.

1397 Same. 1840. Bust; rev., Münich-Augsburg railway. Extremely fine. 24.

1398 BELGIUM. Leopold I. 1849. 2½ Francs; good.

1399 Bust laureate of Leopold I; rev., Agricultural Exposition of Couvin. Very fine, loop removed. 29.

1400 BOLIVIA. 1838. Dollar, bust of Bolivar. Very good.

1401 BRANDENBURG. Frederick III. 1693. ⅔ Crown. Fair.

1402 BRAZIL. 1851, 1855. 500 and 1000 Reis. Uncir. 2 pcs.

1403 BRUNSWICK-LUNEBURG. Charles. 1764. ⅔ Crown. Bust; rev., galloping horse. Very good.

1404 CHILI. 1855. Dollar. Shield in wreath; rev., condor grasping shield. Very good.

1405 ENGLAND. Edward IV. London Groat, *m.m.*, a crown. Good.

1406 Elizabeth. Shilling without date. Bust and shield rather weak, legend sharp. Fine.

1407 Same. 1562, 1592, 1602. Sixpences. Good and very good. 3 pcs.

1408 Charles I. 1625. Nuptial medalet of Charles and Henrietta Maria. Busts facing; rev., Cupid strewing lilies. Fair. 15.

1409 The same. Shilling and Sixpence. Good. 2 pcs.

1410 Oliver Cromwell. Draped bust to left; rev., a lion grasping shield, "Pax qvaeritvr bello." Traces of gilt, good, *rare*. 24.

1411 Charles II. 1670. Crown. Bust; rev., crowned shields, monograms at angles. Lettered edge, good, scarce.

1412 The same. 1663, Shilling; 1679, 4d. Maundy. Fair and fine. 2 pcs.

1413 James II. 1686 and 1687. 4d. Maundy. Good. 2 pcs.

1414 William and Mary. 1689. Half Crown. Good.

1415 William III. 1697. Sixpence. Fair and good. 2 pcs.

1416 Anne. 1707. Bust; rev., crowned shield on altar, crowned lion and unicorn at sides. Very fine. 16.

1417 The same. 1708. Half Crown, E under the bust. Very good.

1418 George I, Sixpence, *South Sea Co.*, fair; George II, 1746, Maundy 4d., fine. 2 pcs.

1419 George III. 1787. Shilling and Sixpence. Bust; rev., square shields, crowns at angles. Uncirculated. 2 pcs.

1420 1804 Bank of England Dollar. Very good.

1421 1805 Bank token; 10 Pence, Irish. Sharp, very fine.

1422 Indian Chief Medal. Bust in armor to right, "Georgius III Dei gratia"; rev., oval shield with motto "Honi soit qui mal y pense" crowned and supported by a crowned lion and unicorn, label inscribed "Dieu est mon droit," roses, shamrocks and thistles beneath. Original loop, very fine and *rare*. 49.

1423 George IV. 1822. Colonial ⅛ and ¼ Crown. Very good. 2 pcs.

1424 1826, Sixpence; 1827, Shilling, type of the crowned lion on crown. Fine and good. 2 pcs.

1425 Victoria. 1853. Gothic Florin. Fine.

1426 The same. 1853, 1857. Gothic Florins. Very good. 2 pcs.

1427 George IV and William IV, Victoria, 3, 4, and 6d. (3); 1858, 20 Cents, Canada. Very good and fine. 6 pcs.

1428 Edward IV, Elizabeth, Charles II, James II, Anne, Henry VIII (Ireland), etc. Penny to Shilling. Fair lot, nine pierced. 21 pcs.

1429 War Medal. Fortress, "Ghuznee"; rev., a mural crown and "23d July 1839" in wreath of laurel. Original clasp (detached) engraved *Afghanistan, Ghuznee*, and *Kelatt, S. Roberts 2d or Queen's Royal.* With ribbon, fine and *rare*. 24.

1430 Engraved Mortuary medals of English rulers, comprising several of the Edwards, Henrys, Richard I, Mary, Elizabeth, Charles and James I and II, etc. Interesting, good to fine, *rare*. 17. 15 pcs.

1431 Mary, Queen of Scotland. 1555. Testoon. Crowned M between crowned thistles, "Maria Dei Gr. Scotor Regina"; rev., arms on cross. Rather poor, a *rare* coin.

1432 Frankfurt. 1844. Gulden. Very good.

1433 FRANCE. Louis XIV, 1707; Louis XV, 1750. Jetons. Former with hand strewing coins on a table, latter a galley on reverse. Fair, both pierced. 18 and 20. 2 pcs.

1434 Louis XVI. 1792. Half Crown. Bust; rev., "Règne de la loi." Fine.

1435 The same. 1793. Crown; rev., Year 5, etc. V. good.

1436 Napoleon I and Josephine. Medallion busts, struck on silver shells. Very fine. 32 to 42. 3 pcs.

1437 Louis Philippe. 1848. 5 Francs. Very fine.

1438 Republic, 1850; Napoleon III, 1852, 1858. Francs. Fine. 3 pcs.

1439. Religious Medal. St. Sebastian tied to an oak and transfixed by arrows; rev., wreath. Octagonal, artistic work. 22.

1440 GERMANY. Bust of Christ; rev., baptismal font in temple. Extremely fine. 27.

1441 Baptismal medal. Baptism of Christ in the Jordan; rev., sponsors holding child at baptismal font. Loop, thin planchet, very fine. 21.

1442 Large group of Cupids emblematic of the various sciences, arts, commerce, and other occupations of man, "Wir sind Alle Gottes Kinder;" rev., Christ on cross, Holy Dove and radiant sun over globe in ornamental circles, "Durch den Glauben." Superb and rare medal. 42.

1443 Friendship Medal. Shields inscribed "Jonathan und David" at foot of an oak tree; rev., hands joined, radiant sign above, German inscriptions. Fine. 36.

1444 Sailors' Medal for Good Luck. St. George slaying the dragon; rev., ship in gale. Fine and scarce, loop. 24.

1445 Ark; rev., Noah and family worshiping at altar, rainbow above. German inscriptions. Very fine. 22.

1446 Radiant triangle over clouds; rev., a crown over communion vessels, German inscriptions. V. fine. 22.

1447 Tablets of commandments; New Year's greetings. German inscriptions. Fine. 17 and 18. 2 pcs.

1448 1730 Ulm Reformation Jubilee. Arms and inscription. Fine. 14.

1449 Munster. 1648. Peace Medal. View of the city, Cupids and the word PAX above; rev., hands joined, cornucopiae, etc. Very fine. 33.

1450 INDIA. One (3), half, and quarter Rupees. Native characters, fine. 7 pcs.

1451 JAPAN. Itzebue (2), and fraction. Oblong square, fine. 3 pcs.

1452 MADRAS. Half Pagoda. Fine, but pierced. 23.

1453 MEXICO. Philip V. 1734. Pillar Dollar. Fine.

1454 Ferdinand VI. 1753. Pillar Dollar. Fine.

1455 Charles IV. 1796. Dollar. Fine.

1456 Religious Medal of St. Teresa of Mexico. Christ on the cross; rev., "Yo soy el camino y la verdad," etc. Oval, loop, extremely fine. 21.

1457 1840 Dollar. Very fine.

1458 Quarter Dollars. Iturbide, 1823; Hook-neck, 1824; the Republic, 1844. Good. 3 pcs.

1459 NETHERLANDS. 1793. Guilder. Figure of Liberty; rev., crowned shield. Very good.

1460 1822 Monument erected to Koster, inventor of the art of printing; rev., inscription. Very fine. 23.

1461 NORWAY. Charles XIV, Johann. 1844. Crown. Bust; rev., crowned arms of Norway in wreath. Very fine impression, but spotted.

1462 The same. 1844. Half Crown. Fine.

1463 PALATINATE. Charles Theodore. 1772. Crown. Very good.

1464 PAPAL. Innocent XII. 1691. Bust; rev., arms. Inauguration medal, original, fine, a little nicked and punctured above head. 23.

1465 PARMA. Maria Louisa. 1815. 5 Lire. Nearly fine.

1466 PERU. 1828. Dollar. Figure of Liberty and arms. nearly fine.

1467 SOUTH PERU. 1838. Dollar. Volcano and tower at sea-shore; rev., radiant sun. Fine.

1468 PORTUGAL. 1818 and 1819. Dollars, for Brazil. Good and fine. 2 pcs.

1469 PRUSSIA. Frederic II, the Great. 1785. Thaler. Very fair.

1470 Frederic William IV. 1841. Double Thaler; fine.

1471 The same. 1846. Double Thaler. Very fine.

1472 PONDICHERRY. Double Fanam. Five lilies; rev., a crown. Thick, fine. 10.

1473 Fanams. Same type, three lilies. Fine, thick. 7. 6 pcs.

1474 Fanams. Similar to last. Good and fine. 5 pcs.

1475 SAXONY. 1610. Triple Crown with bust of Franciscus II, titles as Duke of Saxony, Engadine and Westphalia; rev., crested shield, "Propitio Deo securus ago." Very fine and *rare*. 36.

1476 1610 Four brothers' Crown, two busts facing each other, on each side, the names curiously blended. Good.

1477 1676 John George. Crown. Old bust in armor with drawn sword; rev., shield with eight crests. Fine.

1478 SPAIN. Charles II. Real of Barcelona. Bust in armor with long hair; rev., cross patée, rings and pellets in angles. Fine. *rare.*

1479 Charles IV. 1797. Dollar. Fine.

1480 The same. 1805. Dollar. Very good.

1481 The same. 1807. Dollar. Very fine.

1482 The same. 1808. Dollar. Very fine.

1483 SWEDEN. Gustavus III. 1784. Third Crown. Fine, nicked on edge.

1484 TURKEY. Mustapha III; Abdul Medjid. Dollar and Half Dollar size. Fine and uncirculated, base. 3 pcs.

1485 WURTEMBERG. William. 1818. Kronenthaler. Bust; rev., value under crown, in wreath. Very fine.

1486 The same. 1841. Gulden, 25th anniversary of reign. Very good.

1487 ZURICH. 1813. Crown of 40 Batzen. Cantonal arms; rev., "Domine conserva nos in pace" in wreath. Fine.

1488 College medal. Religion and Faith personified, pointing to college building; rev., view of the completed edifice, "Collegium sancti Edmundi." 1805. Nicked, good. 33.

1489 Cob Medio and Real, France, Prussia, Russia, Spain, Switzerland, Sweden, etc. Silver coins, from Half Dime to Quarter Dollar size. Fine. 18 pcs.

1490 Another lot, includes also Venice, India and Hayti. Fair to good, 7 pierced. 16 pcs.

1491 Base Silver Coins, mostly of German States. Fair to fine. 23 pcs.

FOREIGN COPPER COINS, TOKENS AND MEDALS.

1492 CANADA. Provincial Penny and Halfpenny tokens, Cents, etc. Lot includes several fine Bouquet tokens, J. Roy, T. S. Brown & Co., Magdalen Island token, etc. Fair to uncirculated, many varieties, a desirable lot for selections, 5 pierced. 108 pcs.

1493 1815 Magdalen Island token. Fine. 22.

1494 1812–1820. Penny (2) and Halfpenny tokens, doubtful. Very good and fine. 12 pcs.

1495 Penny token. Bust of Wellington; rev., a Cossack. Very good, scarce.

1496 ENGLAND. James II. 1690. Gun-money half Crown. Very fair.

1497 Carolus a Carolo, William and Mary. Halfp. and Farthings. Fair to very good. 4 pcs.

1498 George III. 1797. Twopence. Slightly nicked on edge, fine. 26.

1499 1797 Twopence. Duplicate of last. Rather poor.

1500 George II to Victoria. Pence and Halfpence. Good to uncirculated. 15 pcs.

1501 Charles II, George I to IV, William IV, Victoria. Farthings. Fair to very fine. 23 pcs.

1502 William IV, ½ Farthing; Victoria, ½ (2), ¼ Far.; Model Crown, Penny (2) and Halfp., gilt and silvered centres. Fine. 8 pcs.

1503 Guernsey. 1830, 4, 1834, 8 Doubles. Very good. 2 pcs.

1504 Tradesmen's Penny Tokens. 1787–1789. Bust of Druid in wreath of oak: rev., monogram. Varieties, very good, scarce. 4 pcs.

1505 1811 Norwich Castle, Newark, Bristol, and South Wales, etc. Good to fine. No duplicates. 22. 6 pcs.

1506 1812 Birmingham Copper Co., Walthamstow, Hull Lead Works. No duplicates. Good and fine. 22. 5 pcs.

1507 1813 Cotton Works at Newcastle, Flint Lead Works, Sheffield, J. Holles, Dublin, Wellington and Erin go bragh. Good to fine. 22. 5 pcs.

1508 Walsall, Barnsley, also J. M. Leigh, Sidney. Penny tokens without date. Very good. 22. 3 pcs.

1509 Tradesmen's Halfpenny Tokens. 1788, 1789, 1790, includes Prince of Wales Masonic. No duplicates. Fine and scarce. 8 pcs.

1510 1791 Druid's head. Varieties, fine and uncir. 4 pcs.

1511 1791 Liverpool, Warwickshire with head of Shakespeare, Gulielmus Tertius, etc. No duplicates, fine. 8 pcs.

1512 1792 Lady Godiva, Lancaster, City of Norwich, Edinburgh, etc. Beautiful impressions, uncirculated, no duplicates. 8 pcs.

1513 1792 All different, no duplicates of last lot, average fine. 11 pcs.

1514 1792 Isle of Wight Halfpenny. Bust of Robert Bird Wilkins; rev., a galley. Uncirculated; *rare.*

1515 1793 York, North Wales, Petersfield, Earl Howe, Shrewsbury, Leeds, Lady Godiva, Birmingham, Norwich, etc. Very fine and uncirculated. No duplicates. 11 pcs.

1516 1793 Another select lot, all different, no duplicates of last, except Lady Godiva Halfpenny. Good to very fine. 11 pcs.

1517 Open volume inscribed "The wrongs of man, Jan 21 1793"; rev., man hanging to gibbet, "End of Pain." nearly proof, *rare.*

1518 1794 Earl Howe, Dundee, Sussex, Northampton, King and Constitution, Newgate, Ipswich, Kent, Loyal Suffolk Yeomanry, etc. No duplicates, uncirculated, desirable. 24 pcs.

1519 1794 All different, no duplicates of last. Good to very fine. 20 pcs.

1520 1794 Lady Godiva on horseback; rev., Coventry cross. Very fine and *rare.*

1521 1794 John Howard, philanthropist; J. H. Tooke, T. Hardy, "Tried for high treason;" Bill of Rights. Fine to uncir. 4 pcs.

1522 1795 Chelsea, Newgate, London Corresponding Society, Sir Jeffery Dunstan, Mayor of Garrat, George, Prince of Wales, etc. No duplicates, uncirculated, desirable. 20 pcs.

1523 1795 All different, no duplicates of last. Fine. 12 pcs.

1524 1795 London Halfpenny token. Bust of George Washington; rev., a grate. Uncirculated, scarce.

1525 1795 Bust of D. I. Eaton; rev., hogs feeding, etc., "Printer to the majesty of the people." Fine, scarce.

1526 1796 Leith, Norwich, Bungay, Sarum Cathedral, etc. No duplicates; very good to uncir. 12 pcs.

1527 1796 Three men hanged to gibbet, "Noted advocates for the rights of men;" rev., "A way to prevent knaves getting a trick." *Brass*, nearly proof, *very rare* halfp. token.

1528 1797 Dudhope Castle, Leith, Stafford, Sir John Jervis defeats Spanish fleet. Fine and very fine, scarce. 4 pcs.

1529 Halfpenny tokens without date, Prince of Wales, Hereford, London and Middlesex, etc. No duplicates; uncirculated. 16 pcs.

1530 Another lot. All different, no duplicates of last. Good to fine. 14 pcs.

1531 Halfpenny tokens, duplicates of preceding Nos. Very good to uncirculated. 12 pcs.

1532 Odd Fellows. Satirical Halfpence. Double face, "Quis rides, Odd Fellows;" another, human and donkey heads combined, "Odd Fellows, a guinea pig, a million hog," etc. All different, fine and uncirculated. 3 pcs.

1533 Spence's Satirical Halfpence. Hog trampling upon a tiara, crown, etc.; rev., "Thos Spence, Sir Thos More, Thos Paine, noted advocates for the rights of man," and another. Sharp and uncirculated. 2 pcs.

1534 Farthing Tokens. Pidcock's Exhibition. Elephant; rev., cockatoo. Uncirculated.

1535 Negro kneeling, "Am I not a man and a brother"; rev., hands clasped. *Rare* and fine halfpenny token.

1536 Duplicate of last: also female kneeling; rev., "United States of America, Liberty, 1838" Fine. 2 pcs.

1537 Farthing Tokens. Negro kneeling, "Am I not a man and a brother," rev., Adam and Eve; another, different reverse. Uncirculated, *rare*. 2 pcs.

1538 Farthing Tokens, Jetons, etc. Copper and brass, good and fine. 8 pcs.

1539 FRANCE. 1792. Monneron token for 5 Sols. Soldiers before Liberty seated: reverse, inscription. Fine. 25.

1540 1848 Essais for 10 Centimes, struck on planchet one quarter of an inch in thickness. Different, mint state. 5 pcs.

1541 SANDWICH ISLANDS. Kamehameha III. 1847. Cent. Fine.

1542 SIERRA LEONE. 1796. Cent. Very good.

1543 Austria, Baden, Brazil, Ceylon (two with elephant), Chili, Dutch India, East India, Ess. and Demerara, France, Gibraltar, India, Guernsey, Japan, Lunenburg, Netherlands, Prussia, Russia, Saxony, Spain, Sweden, Switzerland, Turkey, Utrecht. Fine select copper coins, large and small. 63 pcs.

1544 Miscellaneous Foreign coppers, tokens, etc. Good, 11 pierced. 134 pcs.

1545 English brass weights for coins. Fine. 4 pcs.

1546 Roman Denarius; middle and small bronze. Average poor. 10 pcs.

1547 Roman Catholic medalets, French and English inscriptions, mostly brass. Fine lot. 27 pcs.

1548 British and Foreign Anti-Slavery Society. Varieties of reverses, each with figure of negro in chains. Interesting and scarce. W.m., fine, three pierced. 4 pcs.

1549 Series of portrait medals of French kings, each with bust and inscription. Electros. 22. 61 pcs.

1550 Royal Hawaiian Agricultural Society. Copper, very fine. 40.

1551 Pius IX; Francis of Austria; Edward, Prince of Wales; Napoleon III; Maria II of Portugal; etc. Bronze medals; fine. 17 to 23. 10 pcs.

1552 Titan Vecellius. Bust; rev., female portrait. Gilt electro., very fine. 40.

1553 Christian VII of Denmark. Bust; rev., reception in England, 1768. Bronze, very fine. 24.

1554 England. Oliver Cromwell. Bust by *Dassier*; rev., monument and inscription. Bronze, very fine. 25.

1555 Anne. Bust l.; rev., crowned shield supported by cupids. Bronze, very fine. 22.

1556 George I. Head to right; rev., restitution of the Order of the Bath, 1725. Bronze, fine. 30.

1557 Victoria. 1838. Coronation medal. Bronze, very fine. 24.

1558 France. Henry V. 1830. Pattern for 5 Francs, Copper; very fine.

1559 Prussia. Fred. William III. Bust; rev., commemorates his visit to the French mint, 1814. Bronze, very fine. 26.

1560 Poland. Stanislaus Augustus. 1764. Coronation medal. Head to right; rev., a crown. Red bronze, very fine.

1561 Sweden. Christina. Bust to right; rev., radiant sun, "Nec falso nec alieno." Bronze, very fine. 24.

1562 Joannes Roage, Charles Marquis Cornwallis, Henry the Pious, Droz medal with bust of Charles IV and Augusta. Copper, bronze and gilt. Fine. 22 to 28. 4 pcs.

1563 Bust of Admiral Rodney; rev., "St. Eustatia . Saba and St. Martins taken from the Dutch." Brass, very good. 23.

1564 George III, William IV, Wm. IV and Adelaide, Victoria, Victoria and Prince Albert, Victoria at the Royal Exchange, Nelson, Wellington, Duke of Cambridge, Sir Francis Burdett, Sir I. M. Brunel, Eleanor R. Byrne, etc. W.m., fine, 4 pierced. 21 to 39. 19 pcs.

1565 Britannia sustaining Poland, "Poland thou art not lost;" rev., the "Polish Association," etc. 1833. W.m., fine, *rare*. 26.

1566 Luther's Monument at Worms. W.m. proof. 39.

1567 Copies of rare medals, many of Napoleon I, casts, electros. W.m., etc. 51 pcs.

1568 Electros of rare American medals, also of Washington Half Dollar, Colonial Coins, etc. 23 pcs.

1569 Satirical Medal. Profile of Israelite with donkey's ears, "This is the Jew, which Shakespeare drew," etc; rev., "What d'ye want op ob and dpo" in oak wreath, etc. W.m. with gilt edge or ring and loop. Very fine, curious. 29.

1570 Modern Shekels. Tin, fine. 22. 2 pcs.

1571 John Calvin. Fine portrait by *Bovy*. Bronze shell. 68.

1572 Henry Lee, rev., inscr. for Paulus Hook, 1779; John Paul Jones, rev., ships in action. Bronze shells, struck from dies. Fine. 29 to 36. 2 pcs.

1573 Napoleon III, Aphrodite. Bronze shells, obv. and rev. All different, fine. 27 to 44. 5 pcs.

UNITED STATES COINS.

1574 GOLD DOLLARS. 1853. Very fine.

1575 1854 Uncirculated.

1576 1854 Indian head; very good.

1577 1855 Very good.

1578 1856 Very good.

1579 1857 Very good.

1580 1859 Nicked; very good.

1581 1859 *Charlotte m.* Very good.

1582 1861 Fine.

1583 1862 Fine.

1584 1874 Very fine; scarce.

1585 CENTS. 1794. Poor and fair. 3 pcs.

1586 1795 Plain edge. Fair and good. 3 pcs.

1587 1798 (4), 1800 (2), 1801 (3), 1803 (2), 1805, 1807, 1810, 1814 (2). Fair and very fair. 16 pcs.

1588 1812 Dark; good.

1589 1813 Good; nicked.

1590 1814 Plain 4. Very good.

1591 1817 13 and 15 stars. Fine and good. 2 pcs.

1592 1818 (3), '22 (2), '26, '28 (4), '29, '30 (3), '32, '33 (3), '34. Good and very good. 19 pcs.

1593 1821 Very good, nicked on reverse.

1594 1823 Good for date; scarce. 2 pcs.

1595 1836 Broken die. Very good.

1596 1839 Four varieties. Good. 4 pcs.

1597 1840 Varieties in date. Good. 2 pcs.

1598 1841, '42 (var.), '43, '44 (2), '45 (3), '46 (3), '47 (7), '48 (3), '49 (4), '50, '51 (2), '52 (4), '53 (4), '54 (3), '55 (5), '56 (8). Average fine, several very fine. 53 pcs.

1599 1851 Fine. 9 pcs.

1600 1854 Fine. 7 pcs.

1601 1855 Two with slanting 55. Fine. 9 pcs.

1602 1856 Close and wide date. Fine. 18 pcs.

1603 1857 Large date. Fine. 4 pcs.

1604 1857 Large date. Very good to fine, one with cuts on obverse. 4 pcs.

1605 1857 Large and small date. Fine and very fine. 2 pcs.

1606 1816 to 1857 inclusive. Consecutive; average very good, quite a number fine. 42 pcs.

1607 Cents. Early dates poor, later fair, good and fine. 288 pcs.

1608 Half Cents. 1803, '04 with and without stems to wreath, 1806, '07, '08, '09 (2), 1825, '28, '32 (2), 1835 (4), 1851 (3), 1853, '56, '57. Poor to very fine. 26 pcs.

1609 Two Cents. 1864, '65 (5), 1866, '70, '71. Good to fine. 9 pcs.

1610 Nickel Cents. 1856. Flying eagle. Sharp, nearly proof; very scarce.

1611 1857 (2), 1858, '59 (2), 1863. Fine and uncirculated. 6 pcs.

1612 Three Cents Nickel. 1865 (2), 1881. Fine. 3 pcs.

1613 Colonial Coins. Rosa Am. and Wood ½d., Colonies Françaises, Nova Constel. (3), Vermont, New Jersey (7), Conn. (9), Mass. Cents of 1787 and 1788. Poor to very good. Desirable lot for selections. 30 pcs.

MEDALETS, STORE CARDS, ETC.

1614 Eagle on shield "Massachusetts 1866;" rev., "Lexington April 19, 1775, Baltimore, April 19, 1861" in wreath. Very thick planchet, copper proof, *rare*. 16.

1615 Hon. James Buchanan. Cupid on dolphin; bust of Washington, etc., chiefly with revs. of die-sinkers and coin dealers' cards. Copper, nickel and w.m. Fine to proof., one pierced. 10 to 22. 7 pcs.

1616 Irish Republic; Fenian Brotherhood. Brass and w.m., pierced, uncirculated. 18 and 20. 2 pcs.

1617 Lord Baltimore's Penny, with Wilder's Card. Nickel, bronze, copper, and br. proofs. 14. 4 pcs.

1618 Head of Liberty as on Confed. Cents; rev., R. Lovett Jr.'s Card. Silver, cop. and br. proofs. 12. 3 pcs.

1619 Jacksonian Tokens. Varieties; very good and fine. 5 pcs.

1620 A Cow, "A friend to the Constitution"; rev., ship, "Agriculture and Commerce." Sharp, uncirculated, the finest specimen of this rare token I have seen. 17.

1621 Merchants Exchange; rev., "No. 6 Tontine Building, Wall St." Nickel-plated; uncirculated.

1622 Connecticut. Forbes & Barlow, Water St., New Haven. Very fine. 18.

1623 Dakota Territory. S. E. Ward, Sutler, U. S. A., Fort Laramie. "Good for 50c. in sutler's goods"; rev., blank. Copper, fine. 20.

1624 Illinois. C. Williams, Belvidere: rev., man running, etc. Copper, fair, *rare*. 17.

1625 National Watch Co., Elgin (2); John Plane & Co., Belvidere; A. H. Fisher, Springfield; Willoughby, Hill & Co., Chicago; Pearson & Dana, Chicago. Copper, brass and w.m. Fair to very fine. 16 to 20. 6 pcs.

1626 Kentucky. Sandford Duncan (2); J. W. Quest, Louisville. Cop. and brass. Very fine. 17 and 18. 3 pcs.

1627 Massachusetts. Mahony's 50 Ann St., Boston. Eagle; rev., inscription. Copper, very fine. 18.

1628 Louisiana. Folger & Blake, New Orleans. Eagle; rev., inscription. Good, nickel-plated, *rare*. 18.

1629 N. C. Folger (3); E. Jacobs; L. W. Lyons & Co.; C. Leighton, all New Orleans. Nickel and brass, fine. 15 to 18. 6 pcs.

1630 Eagle grasping key, "Post tenebras lux:" rev., "John A. Merle & Co., Bienville St., New Orleans." Nickel-plated, fine and *rare*. 18.

1631 Missouri. 18th National Saengerfest, St. Louis, 1872. Copper and w.m., (pierced). Fine. 16 and 19. 2 pcs.

1632 View of buildings; rev., "Schnaider's Garden, St. Louis, Mo." German silver, very fine. 21.

1633 M. A. Abrahams, Weston, Mo. Bust, 10 beneath. Brass, fine. 18.

1634 Mermud and Jaccard; W. Pfeiffer; J. E. Esher; Henry J. Kunz; Frank Bochen & Co., all St. Louis. Nickel, brass and w.m. Fair to fine. 10 to 19. 12 pcs.

1635 Scales. "Good at Nicholson's;" rev., "State of Missouri, Half Dime." Nickel, very good, scarce. 10.

1636 Maryland. Keach; A. Knight; Robert Soulsby; Randal & Co. Nickel; very good. 11. 4 pcs.

1637 Mississippi. Eagle with shield, "Benj. F. Fotteral, Vicksburg." Copper, very fine. 18.

1638 Michigan. J. Dimmick, Detroit; David Ball & Co., Foster & Parry, J. W. Pierce, Grand Rapids. Silvered, copper, brass, fine. 13 and 18. 4 pcs.

1639 New York. 1795. Talbot, Allum & Lee, New York Cent. Liberty; rev., ship. Nickel plated, fine. 18.

1640 Park Theatre. 1817. One with "Admit," the other "Paid." Copper, fine, scarce. 13. 2 pcs.

1641 New York. Head of Liberty and 13 stars, 1837; rev., "George A. Jarvis, 142 Grand, cor. of Elm Street, New York," etc. Nearly proof. 18.

1642 Duplicate of last; W. P. Haskins, Troy; James J. Moffet; Phalon's Hair Cutting (2), J. & C. Peck, Troy; Abraham Riker; Robert B. Ruggles. Fine, all size of old copper cent. 8 pcs.

1643 Eagle in circle of stars, 1837; rev., "S. Maywell & Co.," etc. Sharp, extremely fine. 18.

1644 Bradstreet, Hoffman & Co.; rev., "J. M. Bradstreet & Sons, 247 B'way, N. Y." Copper proof. 22.

1645 Bowen & McNamee, 16 William St. (varieties); Benziger Brothers, New York and Cincinnati. Brass, very good and fine. 17 and 18. 3 pcs.

1646 Gould's Saloon, 10 Fulton St., N. Y.; Chesebrough, Stearns & Co. Brass, good and fine. 2 pcs.

1647 Hallock & Bates, 234 Pearl Street, New York; Hallock, Dolson & Bates, 3d door south of Wall Street, New York. Brass, fine, one nicked, *rare.* 19. 2 pcs.

1648 Houghton, Merrell & Co., 48 Cedar St., N. Y.; rev., three parasols. Fine but nicked, nickel-plated. 18.

1649 Dr. J. G. Hewett, bone setter, 68 Prince St., New York; rev., "Practice confined," etc. Copper, fine. 18.

1650 View of old building; rev., Charles D. Hörter, diesinker, 178 William Street, New York, etc. Copper proof. 16.

1651 William G. Jones, Union Coal Office, corner of Chambers and Washington Sts., New York; rev., "Union Coal Yard," etc. Fine, nickel-plated, pierced. 18.

1652 Jennings, Wheeler & Co., 43 Chambers Street, New York, two varieties of reverse. Silvered and brass, very fine. 18. 3 pcs.

1653 Loder & Co.; E. Lyon. Brass and copper, fine and good. 18. 2 pcs.

1654 Leverett & Thomas, 235 Pearl St., New York, "Hardware and Cutlery Goods," etc. Copper, fair, *rare.* 18.

1655 Eagle; rev., a sheaf, "H. Law, Baker, 187 Canal St., New York." Fine and scarce, nickel-plated. 18.

1656 A smoker. "No pleasure can exceed the smoking of the weed"; rev., "Levick, 904 Broadway, New York, 1860," in wreath. W.m., proof, one with name erased. *Rare.* 17. 2 pcs.

1657 M. Leask, 93 Prince St., near Broadway, New York; rev., "Manufacturer of mourning and illusion goods," etc. W.m., very fine, *rare.* 20.

1658 Similar, but "M. Leask, 6 Sands St., Brooklyn, N. Y." W.m., very good, *rare.* 20.

1659 J. C. Merritt, 12 Bowery: Malcolm & Gaul, 62 Liberty St. (2); John Mathews Soda Water Apparatus; Meade & Brother, Albany. Copper and brass, very fine. 18. 5 pcs.

1660 W. H. Mott, corner of Old Slip and Water St., New York: rev., "Dealer in hardware." etc. Brass, good, scarce. 18.

1661 Eagle; "New York Grand Canal, opened 1823": rev., "Tredwel, Kissam & Co., 228 Pearl St., N. Y.," etc. Nickel-plated, good, scarce. 17.

1662 Bust of Indian princess. "United States of America 1860": rev., "F. B. Smith & Hartmann, 122 Fulton St., New York," etc. Nickel proof. 19.

1663 Wood's Minstrels, 563 B'dway, N. Y. Silver, quarter dollar size, very fine.

1664 Woodgate & Co., "Importers of brandies, wines, gins, etc., 83 Water Street, New York 1860"; rev., a shield in circle of stars, "represtd by J. N. T. Levick." Copper proof. 18.

1665 Same as last. Copper proofs. 2 pcs.

1666 Same. Copper proofs. 2 pcs.

1667 Same. Copper proofs. 2 pcs.

1668 Strassburger & Nuhn: Hart & Co.; Doremus & Nixon; Metr. Ins. Co. (2): C. H. Webb; H. B. West; T. Brimmelow, druggist (3). Copper and brass, very fine. 15 to 18. 10 pcs.

1669 Thos. Bennett, 213 Fulton St.; rev., J. C. Bailey, City Hotel, Jersey City. Copper, very fine. 16.

1670 William R. Brown, Saratoga Springs; M. L. Marshall, Oswego; Olcott & Brother, Rochester, N. Y.; Walsh, Lansingburgh. Copper and brass. Fine to proof. 18. 4 pcs.

1671 View of New Congress Hall, 1860, in oval; rev., "Wedding and visiting cards," etc. Silver proof. 16.

1672 Ohio. Dodd & Co., Cincinnati. Bust of Liberty; rev., eagle. Brass, very fine. 18.

1673 Pennsylvania. Bailey & Co., W. A. Drown & Co., W. H. Richardson (varieties,) Sleeper & Fenner, all Phila. Very fine; copper and brass, one silvered. 16 to 19. 5 pcs.

1674 Morse's Literary Depot, Pittsburg; Clark & Anthony, W. A. Hardy, Providence, R. I. Copper, fine. 17 and 18. 3 pcs.

1675 Tennessee. C. G. Cleaves, M. H. Miller & Co., Francisco & Co. (2), Memphis, Francisco & Whitman, Nashville. Copper, brass, fine and very fine. 17 and 18. 5 pcs.

676 South Carolina. Eagle on pestle; rev., "Haviland, Stevenson & Co., Charleston, wholesale druggists, established 1825." Copper, nearly proof. 17.

677 W. W. Wilbur, Charleston (2); I. A. Hopkins, Milwaukee; A. B. Van Cott, Racine, Wis. Cop., very good. 18. 4 pcs.

678 Virginia. S. N. Botsford, Clock and Watch Maker, Norfolk! Beck's Public Baths, Richmond. Copper and composition. Fine and good, (nicked). 18. 2 pcs.

679 Female holding American flag; rev., (engraved.) "Armsted Jackson, Ritchmond, East Va." Tin, good, pierced, *rare*. 16.

680 Copperheads or War Tokens. Lot includes "Coppers 20 per ct. premium;" rev., "A. Ludwig, Pittsburg, Pa." Fine. 22 pcs.

681 Omnibus, Stage, Ferry, and Steamboat Checks. Oval. Nickel, copper and brass, fine, one pierced. 14 to 18. 8 pcs.

682 Encased Postage Stamps. 1 Cent; rev., "Ayers Sarsaparilla to purify the blood" (3); "S. Steinfeld, 70 Nassau St., N. Y., French Cognac Bitters" (1); Shells, Stamps missing (2). Scarce. 6 pcs.

683 3 Cents. "Ayers Sarsaparilla" (3); John Shillito & Co., Cincinnati; Burnett's Cocoaine. One damaged, scarce. 5 pcs.

684 10 Cents; rev., "J. Gault pat. Augus 12, 1862." *Rare.*

685 Medal, Store Cards, Brass Calendar, Metallic Shells, Souvenir, etc. Mostly brass and of the West; a good lot for selections. 13 to 56. 36 pcs.

686 Rubber and papier maché cards. A fine lot. 23 pcs.

687 Collection of Copperheads or War Tokens, mostly of Ohio, Indiana, Michigan, Wisconsin and other Western States. Copper and brass, free of duplicates, nearly all bright, sharp and uncirculated, desirable. 1201 pcs.

688 Foreign Copper Coins. Brazil, England, France, Germany, Italy, India, Mexico, Russia, etc. Mostly large; very good. 100 pcs.

689 Another Selection. Large and small. Very good. 150 pcs.

1690 Canada. Provincial Penny and Halfpenny tokens. Duplicates, several scarce types in lot; average very good. 75 pcs.

1691 Canada. Similar; average very good. 75 pcs.

1692 Canada. Similar; average very good, 9 pierced. 75 pcs.

1693 Miscellaneous copper Coins, includes China, etc. Poor, fair and good, the latter pierced. 126 pcs.

1694 Billon and nickel Coins, Seal, shell Placque. Fair to fine, one pierced. 18 pcs.

1695 Denarius of Gordianus Pius; bronze coins of Rome. Poor to good. 17 pcs.

1696 Ptolemy. Head of Jupiter; rev., eagle. Poor. 26.

NUMISMATIC LITERATURE, MEDALS, ETC.

1697 John Yonge Akerman. Ancient Coins of Hispania, Gallia, Britannia. 24 plates. London, 1846, 8vo, cloth.

1698 American Journal of Numismatics. 8vo, New York and Boston, 1866–1878. Serial Nos. 1 (2), 3, 4, 14, 23, 24, 26, 27, 28, 30, 32, 33, 34, 35, 45, 46, 48, 75, 76, 78, 79. 22 parts.

1699 Michel Chevalier. On the probable fall of the value of gold, etc. Translated from the French by Richard Cobden. New York, 1859, 8vo, cloth.

1700 Decimal Coinage, etc. London, 1753, 8vo, paper cover.

1701 George G. Evans. History of the U. S. Mint and American Coinage. Plates. Philadelphia, 1886, 8vo, cloth.

1702 Mason's Coin and Stamp Collectors' Magazine, Coin Chart Manuals, etc. A bundle.

1703 Numismatic Hand Book. Text in old Dutch characters. Illustrated. The Hague, 1606, small 8vo, paper cover.

1704 W. C. Prime. Coins, Medals and Seals, Ancient and Modern. 114 plates. New York, 1861, small quarto, cloth.

705 James Ross Snowden. A description of Ancient and Modern Coins in the Cabinet Collection at the Mint of the United States. 26 plates in metallic colors and autographic dedication. Phila., 1860, 8vo, cloth.

706 Alfred Sandham. Coins, Tokens and Medals of Canada. Plate. Montreal, 1869, 8vo, cloth.

707 W. E. Woodward. Priced Coin Sale Catalogues. 1863, Oct. 20–24; 1880, Oct. 13–16; 1884, Oct. 13–18. 3 catals.

708 W. E. Woodward. Unpriced Coin Sale Catalogues 1865–1889. 7th Semi-annual Sales, Nos. 20, 23, 24, 26, 28, 30, 31, 33, 34, 36, 40, 42, 44, 52, 55, 67, 89 (2), 90, 93, 94 (2), 95, 97, 98, 99, 101, 102, 103, 106. 31 catals.

1709 Unpriced Coin Sale Catalogues. Boban (Archaeological.) Chubbuck, Edwards, Hawkins, Parker, Parmelee, Taylor, Stenz, Snow, etc. Several early sales in lot. 31 catals.

1710 M. L. Mackenzie, New York, 1869. Plates, priced.

1711 Lorin G. Parmelee, New York, 1873. Plates, priced.

1712 Edward Cogan, Governor Parker, Emil Cauffman, 1871; James B. Clemens, 1878; etc. All priced. 6 catals.

1713 Chapman, Frossard, Low, Proskey, etc. Priced. 7 catals.

1714 Lewis J. Cist. Autographs, Part I. New York, 1886. Priced.

1715 Edward Cardwell. Lectures on the Coinage of the Greeks and Romans. Oxford, 1832, 8vo, cloth.

1716 Joannes Harduin. Nummi Antiqui populorum et urbium. Paris, 1684. Quarto, vellum.

1717 Joannes Vaillant. Numismata Imperatorum Augustorum et Caesarum, etc. Paris, 1698. Quarto, old calf.

1718 Catalogues Numismatum, etc. Ratisbon, 1773. Small 8vo, boards.

1719 Edward Cogan. Coin Sale Catalogues, priced. 1868, Nov. 1; 1873, May 19–21; 1878, Feb. 27, 28, Sept. 16–20; Oct. 22–25; 1879, May 1 and 2, May 29, June 20, Sept. 2 and 3, Dec. 1 and 2. 10 catalgs.

1720 Cohen's Plates of Roman Coins, etc. 40 plates.

A FEW MISCELLANEOUS MEDALS.

1721 George II. 1736. Figure of Minerva; rev., queen watering a plantation of trees. The Cistern Medal. Silver, very good. 25.

1722 War Medal to Palmetto Regiment, S. C. Troops landing, "Vera Cruz, Contreras, Churubusco, Chapultepec, Garita de Belen," on border; rev., shields resting against a Palmetto tree "To the Palmetto Regiment," etc. Silver, without name on label, very fine and *rare*. 31.

1723 1796 Castorland token. Silver proof, restrike from the French mint. 22.

1724 George Washington. Undraped bust to left "The defender of his country;" rev., "May our country never want props," etc. in border of rays and stars. Silver proof. 18.

1725 George Washington. Military bust, 13 stars on border; rev., same bust, 35 stars on border. Silver proof. 18.

1726 Bombardment of Fort Sumter, 1861; rev., inscription. Silver, nearly proof. 22.

1727 Man hanging to gibbet, "Jefferson Davis, 1861;" rev., "Death to traitors." Silver, nearly proof. 16.

1728 1876 Centennial Commission Medal. Silver, very fine. 24.

1729 Major André. Bust; rev., old Dutch church at Tappan, where he was tried. Bronze, extremely fine. 22.

1730 1880 Tarrytown Centennial, with copy of medal awarded captors of André. Bronze, extremely fine. 22.

1731 1859 Pattern Half Dollar. Head of Liberty; rev., "½ Dollar" in broad wreath. Copper, very fine.

1732 London. Elephant Halfp. token. Elephant; rev., arms of London. Good.

1733 Hard Times Tokens. Narrow-shouldered Jackson and three other varieties. Very good. 4 pcs.

1734 Chicago medal. 1871. View of the burning city; rev., a phoenix rising from the pyre. "Made from Chicago Court-house bell." Very fine. 33.

1735 Bronze medal. Barbaric bust, "Attila Rex;" rev., view of city "Aquileia" above. Fine. 27.

1736 France. Louis XIV. 1660. Youthful bust; Cupid driving quadriga on which youthful queen is seated. Bronze, extremely fine. 40.

1737 Louis XIV. 1662. Draped bust laureate; rev., radiant sun over globe "Nec pluribus impar." Bronze, fine, original. 24.

1738 Princess Charlotte. Bust to left; rev., "Son coeur est un écho des vertus de sa mère." Bronze, mint state. 33.

1739 Bust of Frederic von Schiller; rev., (German) "Centennial of birth, N. Y., 1859." W.m., fine. 26.

1740 1792 Monneron token for 5 sols; French Rep., 5 centimes, year 7 and 9; St. Helena Halfpenny, 1821. Very good. 4 pcs.

1741 1794 Lady Godiva Halfp. token, with Coventry cross on reverse. Very good.

1742 1790 Russia. 5 Kopecs. Fine. 27.

1743 Sweden. Charles XII. 1715–1719. Set of copper Dalers; complete, very fine. 16. 10 pcs.

1744 1718 Spanish Two Reals; 1883, Mexico, Nickel Cent; Mexican Bank, 25 Centavos. 3 pcs.

1745 Roman Aes and Sextans, reduced size. Poor and fair. 2 pcs.

NUMISMATIC BOOKS, PAMPHLETS, ETC.

1746 Am. Journal of Numismatics. Boston, 1873–1889. Serial Nos. 61–121 from July, 1873 to July, 1888, consecutive: also No. 123, January, 1889. Fine condition. 62 Nos.

1747 Am. Num. and Arch. Society of New York. Proceedings and papers, 29th annual meeting. 8vo, paper, N. Y., 1887.

1748 D. J. Henr. Burckhard. Numophylacium Burckhardianum. Describes Antique Coins, Thalers and Ducats, Medals, Brunswick-Luneburg Coinage, etc. Helmaestadt, 1740, small quarto, boards, bound into one volume.

1749 Catalogue of Ancient and English Coins, etc. of Thos. Hollis. 8vo, half mor., London, 1817, priced.

1750 Catalogue of Greek and Roman Coins, sold in London, 1844. 8vo, half mor., priced and named.

1751 Dr. M. W. Dickeson. American Numismatical Manual. Quarto, 19 plates, Philadelphia, 1859.

1752 J. Evelyn. A Discourse of Medals Antient and Mod rn, etc. London, 1697, small folio, old calf.

1753 Marquard Herrgott. Monumenta Augustae Domus Austriacae. Text profusely illustrated with plates of seals, coats of arms, medals and coins of Dukes, Archdukes and Emperors of the Imperial and other noble houses of Austria. Frontispiece to each volume. Folio, Vienna and Friburg, 1750–1752, half russia, binding somewhat broken, but work perfect; stamped as a duplicate from the British Museum, 1831. 3 vols.

1754 John A. Hickcox. An Historical account of American Coinage. Albany, 1858, Imperial 8vo, half calf, gilt top.

1755 Joannes Harduin. Antirrheticus de Nummis Antiquis. Paris, 1689. Quarto, plates, old calf.

1756 J. P. von Ludewig. Einleitung zu dem Deutschen Münzwesen mittlerer Zeiten. Ulm, 1752, 12mo, half calf, plate.

1757 Miscellaneous Autographs. 4 pcs.

1758 Miscellaneous plates, Engravings, etc., some rare and valuable. 52 pcs.

1759 Manuscript Catalogue of English Coins, Coins of Cunobeline, Folkes' Tables of gold coins, Coins of Canute and other works and pamphlets, published in England, 1708–1774, and bound in one volume, half calf, binding loose.

1760 Numismata Aerea Selectiora Maximi Moduli e Museo Pisano olim Carrario. Vol. I, 92 plates of Antique Coins, Medallions, etc. Folio, old calf, *rare*, once sold for £7 7sh.

1761 Paolo Pedrusi. I. Cesari in Oro, racolti nel Farnese Museo. Parma, 1694–1727. Folio, vellum. Many full page illustrations. A rare and valuable work. 10 vols.

1762 Alfred H. Satterlee. Medals and Tokens, of the Presidents of the United States. New York. 1862, 8vo, cloth.

1763 Silber-Münzen von Nürnberg. Part I, comprising Thalers, Gulden, etc. Nurnberg. 1766, large 8vo, half mor., numerous cuts.

1764 Theodore Toussenel. Précis Chronologique de l'histoire de France. Quarto, imitation morocco. Paris, 1844. with plates of French Kings.

1765 Views in Glasgow and Neighborhood, lithographed by David Allan. Glasgow, 1835, oblong folio. 10 plates.

1766 Henry Whitfield. Strength out of Weakness or a Glorious Manifestation of the further progress of the Gospel among the Indians of New England. Original manuscript, complete. New York, 1865.

1767 J. Vaillant. Numismata Imperatorum Augustorum et Caesarum, etc. Amsterdam. 1700. Cuts and plates. Folio, vellum.

1768 J. Vaillant. Historia Ptolemaeorum Aegipti Regum. Amsterdam, 1701. 152 plates and cuts. Folio, vellum.

1769 J. Vaillant. Nummi Antiqui Familiarum Romanarum, etc. Amsterdam, 1703. Frontispiece, folio, vellum. 2 vols.

1770 J. Vaillant. Numismata Imperatorum Romanorum praestantiora a Julio Caesare ad Postumum usque, etc. Roma, 1743, quarto, vellum. 3 vols.

1771 Document or Conveyance on parchment, issued in the year 1784, during the reign of George III. Fairly preserved.

1772 Japanese Lance. Lacquered staff, with sharp curving blade. 8 feet.

1773 Japanese Sword. With guard and sheath.

1774 United States Springfield Musket. Used during the Rebellion.

1775 Flint-lock Pistol. Slightly imperfect. 14 in.

1776 Duelling Pistol. In perfect order.

1777 Old Bayonet. War of 1812.

1778 Engraved Metallic Beaker. Curious form.

1779 Dr. Winslow Lewis's Coin Cabinet of black walnut. Contains twenty drawers, each lined with black velvet and half an inch deep. Covered with an Italian marble slab bevelled and polished. Size 41 x 31 x 24 in. A fine cabinet for collectors or dealers.

1780 Black Walnut Cabinet. Formerly the property of H. W. Holland of Boston, which contained his superb collection of American Medals, especially full in those relating to the Presidents and Presidential candidates. Contains forty-eight velvet lined drawers, each 15½ x 13 in., and from ½ to ¾ in. deep. Top opens for large medals.

ANNOUNCEMENT.

The undersigned begs to announce that he holds frequent sales by auction in New York and Boston, of coins, medals, tokens and pre-historic objects in stone and flint, pottery, bronze and copper, and solicits consignments of the same from collectors, and owners, executors, administrators and trustees, all of which goods he will properly catalogue, and offer for sale to a large constituency of buyers both in America and in Europe with a view to obtaining for owners remunerative prices.

To the sale of coins and medals particularly, and of the various objects to which collectors turn their attention he has devoted his time for more than thirty years, and he feels that the multitude of his sales and the general success attending them offer a guarantee of faithful service.

For this service a uniform charge of 25 per cent. is made with such trifling expense as packing boxes and transportation, which is seldom more on a consignment than from one to two dollars. This commission includes preparation of the catalogue, printing, distribution and postage, and attendance on the sale in the interest of owners, and purchases made free of commission to buyers, with no charge to them except freight and packing as aforesaid.

Aware of the low prices at which sales are undertaken at auction, it may be said that the average cost of auction sales for cash paid out averages about 17 per cent. and it is obvious that it cannot fairly be undertaken for less than 25, and in case it is, some interest of the owner must be neglected either by inadequate description or by crowding lots together at the risk of realizing inadequate prices.

W. ELLIOT WOODWARD,
258 Dudley Street,
Roxbury, Mass.

www.ingramcontent.com/pod-product-compliance
Lightning Source LLC
Chambersburg PA
CBHW032249080426
42735CB00008B/1064

* 9 7 8 3 7 4 3 3 4 1 9 2 0 *